I Shall Live And Not Die

By

Nadeen Brown

I Shall Live And Not Die

All scripture verses used for this book were referenced from the NKJV version of the Bible.

Some of the names mentioned in this book have been either changed or abbreviated to protect the privacy of the individuals.

The information shared in this book about mental and emotional healing is entirely based on the author's experience and is not intended to take the place of a certified mental health counselor or medical practitioner.

Editor: Janelle C. Simmons
Reader: Kimberley Morrison
Book Illustrator: Bob Buel

IBSN-10-0615513751
ISNB-13-9780615513751
Printed in the United States of America

Acknowledgements

°∞°∞°∞°∞°∞°∞°∞°∞°

Praise the Lord for the incredible grace He has poured upon me to write this book within a short period of time! Special thanks to Staffany Smith, who believed that I had a story to share with the world, that would encourage the hearts of many, even long before I conceived the idea of writing this book. Special thanks to Michael Sparman for his friendship and legal consultation in writing this book. I am also grateful to my mother, Millicent Brown, for nurturing my potential to write, sister, Shari Brown and friends Joy Payne Phillips, Angelica Fowler, Shirley Darroux, Kavitha Paranjothi, Sharon Lindsey, Shirley Hendricks, Dr. Judy Duncker; prayer partners, Londye Dorleus and Medline Altenor; and Christ Church's Intercessory ministry for their encouragement, love, support and prayers that kept me going.

I extend heartfelt gratitude to the Editor, Janelle C. Simmons, the Reader, Kimberley Morrison and the Book Illustrator, Bob Buel.

Table of Contents

Introduction

°∞°∞°∞°∞°∞°∞°∞°∞°

It was Friday and the end of a work week. Anyone that works Monday through Friday usually looks forward to the weekend. Teachers have one of those professions that require ongoing planning and preparation at home. School had just resumed from the summer break and the fullness of the school schedule did not take effect just yet. So for me, this was going to be a light work weekend. That alone was enough to celebrate and I was going to enjoy my weekend.

I quickly shifted focus from my professional concerns, challenges and expectations for the new group of students I was responsible for that school year. Filled with excitement and anticipation for the weekend finally arriving, I went over in my mind the endless possibilities of spending time with my family and friends as I walked out of my work building.

The skies were blue and not one rain cloud was in sight. There were only a few white clouds which formed beautifully fluffed pillow patterns across the skies as the afternoon sun shone with brilliance. It was a perfect day. The trees rustled each time there was an occasional light wind. Everyone was out soaking up the sun. Like man, the birds were enjoying the day. Flocks of birds were flying south, while others were flying in and out of tree tops, filling the air with melodious chirping.

Breathing in the fresh fall air created an internal surge of energy that heightened my appreciation for nature. I loved such experiences with nature because they always helped me to connect with God. Enjoying the moment, I marveled at how God communicates His splendor to mankind through the works of His hands as I considered the galaxies, planets, sun, moon, stars, earth, all life forms and the different seasons. God's vastness is limitless! Who can comprehend such greatness? As I became one with nature, I experienced tranquility and an overwhelming gratitude to God. I uttered praise unto God inwardly. God's love was evident, through the peace that flooded my soul. I felt great!

Walking leisurely to the parking lot, I enjoyed a lighthearted conversation with one of my colleagues whose car was parked adjacent to mine. After lingering for a few more moments of conversation and laughter, we finally parted. I placed my bags into the trunk and got into my car. Immediately, I started channel surfing to find some upbeat contemporary Christian music, but I eventually settled for one of my old favorite lively worship CDs. I cranked the volume dial to the highest tolerable decibel. I was definitely ready for a great time. I thought of a friend who once said to me that he never has to take drugs to get high because music is his high. In that moment, music was my high! As I settled in my car seat, I rolled the windows down and opened the sun roof. I could also hear a mix of music thumping from cars that were passing.

As I drove, I could see that some people were having barbeques in their backyards. The air was filled with grill smoke, fun, laughter and music. Other people were either sitting on their porches or outside in their yards. This was nostalgic.

In Jamaica, it was not uncommon, especially in the countryside for people to sit outside in their yards in the afternoon while families ate together, swapped stories, laughed, encouraged one another; played, imparted wisdom and offered solid counsel. This breathes a sense of family unity, which strengthens the overall fabric of the family unit. Quality family time helps children feel secure. It is amazing how this type of family involvement makes a tremendous difference in a child's life.

As I drove through the neighborhood, it reminded me of the simplicity of life in the Caribbean. I could feel the wind through my hair as the air of freedom hugged and kissed my face while I sped down the freeway. I was exceptionally joyful. There was not a stressful thought that had entered my mind as I reflected on my weekend itinerary… going to the movies, dinner, theater, hanging out at the Christian Café or simply connecting with family and close friends. Lost in my thoughts, I did not care which order the weekend events unfolded, I was in full anticipation. Moments later, I pulled into my driveway.

Awakened from future expectations to reality, I was home. I quickly gathered my bags and walked briskly towards my apartment. I opened the front door, checked my mailbox in the vestibule of the building and proceeded up four flights of stairs to my corner apartment. There was no one in sight. This was not unusual. Practically all the residents in the complex worked during the day. The empty hallways echoed the sounds of my loud clanging shoes and rustling keys. Aware of my surroundings but not cautious, I stood before my apartment door, bags in one hand and my keys in the other. I was moments away from entering a journey that would change my life forever!

Chapter 1

°∞°∞°∞°∞°∞°∞°∞°∞°

Refusing To Die

Friday, September 14, 2007, my life changed! It was about three in the afternoon. I had no set time to be home, but due to a Pep Rally held early in the afternoon at my school, there was an early dismissal, so I was home earlier than usual. In the hallways leading up to my apartment, no one was in sight. Just like any other day, I placed my keys in the lock and opened my apartment door. With the door slightly cracked, I was about to enter my apartment, when the unexpected happened. It was like a scene from a riveting Hollywood movie that was unfolding in that very moment and I was one of the main actors. With my bags in one hand and the other hand turning the keys in the door, I was about to enter my sanctuary of peace and serenity. But suddenly, a young man jumped out of the vacant apartment across the hall. He was dressed in a black leather jacket and blue denim pants. He had on a black ski-mask covering his face and black leather gloves covering his hands. He grabbed me from behind and held me in a neck hold, with a kitchen knife blade at my throat. It was an unreal moment. I could feel the knife blade pressing against my neck. My heart was pounding as I felt the massive throbbing of my carotid arteries. My throat was parched and my tongue heavy from shock. It was a moment in which one would want to wake up and say;

"Thank God! This was only a bad dream."

I waited, but it was not. It was very real! Immediately, my body went into the flight/fight response mode when I realized the extent of the travesty ahead, if my attacker should succeed in getting me into the apartment. I started pushing back, trying to remain in the hallway. I thought my chances for obtaining help or fighting back would be greater in the hallway than inside my apartment. However, my attacker was about six feet and three inches tall at 220 pounds. He was solid in shape and form, and my natural strength was no match for his. He quickly shoved me into my apartment and locked the door before I even had time to react. I shuddered, as the door slammed shut which evoked fear that sent chills up my spine. At that moment, I stepped into a zone of 'NO RETURN.' Caught in a fight for my life, I started screaming;

"Jesus! Jesus! Jesus! Help! Help!"

It felt as if I were calling from 100 feet under the earth. I realized that this cry was of no avail. In a sound-proof apartment and with everyone at work; no one was going to hear me. At that moment, in desperation, I said;

"Jesus, only you can deliver me!"

This was when I remembered my pastor once told us a story about another pastor and his elders who were having their weekly prayer meeting when God revealed a vision to one of the men. The man saw that a young woman was being attacked and immediately the pastor sent help for the young woman and started to intercede on her behalf. In a state of despair, I breathed and prayed in my mind;

"God I sure hope you have someone praying for me now. I need prayer."

Held in a neck hold position, he forced me to lie down on the floor by the door of my apartment.

"Lay down, lay down," he repeated, as he forced me to submit.

I knew I could not lie down because it would cost me too much. Without thinking about the ramifications of denying his requests, I knew that if I laid down I was going to die one way or another, whether psychologically or physically. Tenacity rose in me. FORGET THAT! I am not going to lay down for this animal to have his way with me.

As he grabbed my clothing, forcing me on the floor, I realized his intentions were to rape me. Every day that week I wore wide flowing skirts to work, except that day. I wore the perfect attire. A black blouse tucked in a slim fitting pair of black pants which was secured with a front zipper and reinforced by clasps. I reflected on how amazing God was.

As I was preparing my clothes for work the night before, I could not decide whether I should wear a skirt or pants. So, I started praying to the Lord about what He would have me wear. This, too, was odd for me because I don't make a habit of always praying about what to wear. Strange but divine... I finally felt a peace about wearing pants. Little did I know that my choice of clothing would help in sparing me from being raped.

So, I started fighting back, as hard as I could. I had to! I refused to let this man take my virtue. As a young Christian woman, I was set aside by the Lord and take delight in how the Lord has graced me to offer my body as a living sacrifice... holy and acceptable in His sight. As I matured in Christ, I truly wanted to reserve the deepest part of myself as an ultimate expression of my love for my husband. I refused to be taken without a fight!

The attacker, did not bargain for this either. I could hear the frustration in his tone as he laced his commands with expletives. I imagined he did not expect me to fight back the way I did. He was bitterly mistaken. He thought that because I had a slender frame, I would be an easy target. However, he did not know that I was involved in moderate strength training. Moreover, I grew up on a farm doing manual labor.

As the struggle persisted, I recognized the attacker. Although he had his face covered, the holes around the eyes of the ski mask were larger than normal and revealed his cheekbone structure along with other facial details. Imagine the shock! Why would he want to kill me? Why would he try to hurt me like this? I never did anything to offend this man. I was no stranger to him. Why did he want to unleash such evil towards me?

It turned out that he was one of the maintenance workers in the building. There were many times that I would pass him in the hallways cleaning or tending to the upkeep of the apartment complex. I was always cordial.
In fact, a few months earlier while him and his supervisor were working on the plumbing system in my apartment, I spoke with the attacker's boss, within his ear reach, in regards to why God was so concerned about our hearts. Recently, I led a small bible study discussion

about the heart so I had been well prepared. As I ministered to his boss, the Holy Spirit revealed the following;

"The heart is the center of life. It is the essence of who we are as people. The heart is the seat of our being. It is the place where wickedness is conceived before it comes forth. God knows this and wants us to give Him our hearts, so that He can transform us as He removes the impurities that block the flow of His Spirit in and through us. Similarly, physically it is critically important to keep the blood vessels of the heart clear, to ensure that adequate blood supply with oxygen and nutrients would be delivered to vital organs in the body. This is necessary in maintaining life. Therefore, we must repent of impure and sinful patterns because they cause spiritual death."

Locked in the awesome revelation of God and the great work the Spirit of God was accomplishing, I went on to tell his boss the following;

"We don't have to experience spiritual death because of what Christ did on Calvary. All we have to do is repent and turn to Him. God will give us hearts of flesh in exchange for our stony hearts."

Concluding the conversation, I offered to pray for both men that day. I specifically prayed that God would cleanse their hearts including mine, so that we could be counted as righteous ones.

"Who shall ascend into the hills of the Lord? Or who may stand in His holy place? He who has clean hands and a pure heart...He shall receive blessing from the Lord, and righteousness from the God of his salvation." -Psalm 24:3-5

I cried out to the Lord in a moment of powerful intercession that God would purge our hearts. Closing the prayer, I prayed for God to bless the attacker and his boss. Later, both men finished their work in my apartment and left.

I would have never thought that the next time I would see this young man, he would be attacking me. Although I was perplexed as to the reason for the attack, the reality of death was eminent. I wondered to myself, if he succeeded in killing me, who would tell the police what he did?

As the attack unfolded, he pressed the knife against my throat and did not let up. I saw my life flashing before me. I was in disbelief. I never imagined that I would die like this. I anticipated being married, having children, traveling the world and ushering in the presence of God in worship. I could see myself going on mission trips, building my greeting card business, writing books, making lots of money and growing old in the Lord and eventually enjoying my grandchildren. An early death was not a part of the equation. In dismay, my heart pounded. I cried out;

"I can't believe that I am going to die like this. Am I really going to be murdered in my own apartment?"

I could not bear the image of my family finding my lifeless bloody body on the floor of my apartment. This grief would be too much for my Mom, Dad, siblings and close friends. I saw my funeral and the rain clouds hanging over the procession. I could hear the words of remembrance as people recounted who I was and what I had done. Better yet, I could hear the words of some who were noting the potential I had to do great things for God. I saw the black veils and the sorrow that overwhelmed the hearts of the mourners.

Although being absent from the body is to be present with the Lord, I had a difficult time accepting an early death. I was only thirty years old! I had not started life yet! There was so much I had not accomplished yet. In fact, like a tape, all the prophetic words spoken over my life, started playing in my mind. None of it said early death! All those words spoke of hope, longevity and blessings.

As my spirit took a stance of refusing to die, my stomach churned and almost indignantly, I said to God;

"This is not what the prophetic word said about my life. This cannot be it! I cannot be a blessing to anyone dead! Change that script! God, this is not what you said! I will not die!"

Instantaneously, the scriptures bubbled up in my belly, and I was empowered with the tenacity to fight and live, like never before. Inwardly, I purposed;

"I shall not die, but live,
And declare the works of the Lord!"
-Psalm 118:17

The word of God welled up in me, as the Spirit of God connected with my spirit and a supernatural strength came upon me. I fought more intensely. I got out of the neck hold position my attacker had me in and I was able to grab a hold of the knife handle over his hand as I wrestled to get the knife away from my throat.

As the struggle ensued, I was pushed backwards and fell on my back. This was the worst position to be in, but with my adrenaline firing, I was not going to give up! Caught between the battle of life and death, the knife struggle became even more intense. Aiming the knife away from my throat, for several moments, we pointed the knife back and forth at each other. I was determined he was not going to slit my throat. Although I was trusting, fighting and praying; I knew that I needed deliverance. In one gridlock moment, the knife was only a millimeter from penetrating my throat. This was when I believed that the heavens opened up and the demonstrative power of God was released. Empowered by the Spirit of the Living God, I pushed the knife handle with every fiber of my being, and emphatically breathed out the words...

"I shall live and not die!"

Instantly, the knife miraculously broke into two! The blade had separated from the handle and fell in a corner somewhere and my attacker could not find it. Later that evening, when the police tried to retrieve the knife from the crime scene, they could not find it. It was my mother who actually found the knife and showed it to the police. No one would have just been able to find the blade, especially my attacker who was trying to find it in a hurry.

In my mother's report to the police, she marveled as she described how the knife blade was neatly pressed against the wall by a stack of boxes that I had bought for my greeting card business. Even as recent as the day before the attack, I remember looking at the stack of boxes, shaking my head and saying;

"Lord why did I ever waste my money to buy these boxes that I never use?"

The next day, I was so grateful that I bought those boxes, because they helped to conceal the knife, which in turn saved my life. This was beyond any story of fiction. The one who saved me was the King of Kings, the Lord of heaven and earth and the ever powerful, omnipotent God Almighty. He showed up for me in the nick of time.

The attacker had been dismayed. I could tell he was extremely frustrated as he cursed. Soon his frustration led to another level of fury. Being weaponless and refusing to leave me alive, he came upon me and straddled the upper part of my body with his legs, grabbed my neck with his bare hands and started to squeeze my throat. Although I fought immensely, by kicking my legs, pushing and clawing to break free from his hold. He was in an advantageous position, which made it easy for him to overpower me. As the attacker crouched over my incapacitated body, his eyes glared the hateful intent of his heart. His fingers pressed into my neck. It became difficult for me to breathe. I was grasping for air. My chest heaved as my breathing became laborious which was accompanied by choking and gargling sounds. With my tightly clenched fists, I fought for my life. But soon my hands fell to my side and my forceful kick weakened. My legs fell lifeless as the last ounce of air oozed from my body and I could no longer breathe. Within moments everything became black and my body laid still on the floor.

Believing that I was dead, my attacker took my hand bag and left my body on the floor. In that moment, I believed that the death angel visited me and my spirit separated from my body. I do not recall exactly how long my listless body laid on the floor, but God, the Life Giver said;

> "No, it is not your time to come home. I have work for you to do."

I believe that the angels of the Lord resuscitated me and within moments I woke up. I could not recall who I was, where I was or what had happened.

Chapter 2

°∞°∞°∞°∞°∞°∞°∞°∞°

Trauma

Everywhere was pitch-black. In a semiconscious state, I felt as if I had been in a plane crash. My head hurt and my throat was unbearably parched. I just wanted to get out of this situation. Miraculously, I was able to get out of the apartment and descended four flights of steps, after being unconscious for some time. God promises to give His angels charge over us to keep us in all ways. As I reflect, I believe that only angels could have lifted me down those stairs. By the time I arrived at the lobby of the building, a woman saw me bleeding and screamed;

"Someone call 911. She is hurt!"

I continued outside the building, with a muddled mind, as I floated in and out of consciousness, I cried;

"OW did it!"

My clothes were ripped. I can only imagine that my hair was a mess. I also had blood all over me. By the time I was outside of the building, people were gathering around me and asking me what had happened. I felt as if a thousand bricks had fallen on me and I was going to pass out. I just wanted to lie down. Deeply distressed, I cried hysterically. By then a crowd of people gathered around me. I heard someone say;

"The ambulance is on its way."

Another person said;

"The property manager started chasing OW, when he saw him running from the building a few minutes before she came outside."

The police came and started interrogating me. I did my best to answer the questions but I was just hanging on by a thread. The tears were streaming down my face. I just wanted someone to hold me. I cried like a baby. I needed my mother, family and loved ones. The reality of the incident was unbearable. I bent over in the walkway and sobbed uncontrollably. The police kept bombarding me with questions. It was as if no one realized I was fatigued. I could hardly stand. No one came forward to hold my hand or offered any other type of support. I needed to be comforted. I sobbed in my hands,

"God, why can't these people around me, help me? Everyone is so focused on getting the facts, they forgot that I survived."

The shock from the trauma began settling in my body. I felt myself being lolled into a deep sleep. I needed prayer. I wished one of the people that gathered around me that knew how to pray would pray. Of course, that was not the case. So, I started to pray silently. My thoughts were so jumbled, I had no strength and my words made no sense. God was my only source and so I pressed in, focusing on the power of God as much as I could. Psalm 91 came into my mind.

"He that dwells in the secret place of the most high, shall abide under the shadow of the Almighty, I will say of the Lord, He is my refuge and my fortress." -Psalm 91:1-2

As I continued to recite Psalm 91, the Holy Spirit ministered strength to my inner man to hold on. Finally, the ambulance came, and I was strapped onto the stretcher. I wanted to sleep. Before the EMT could finish checking my vital signs, my mother came.

Interestingly enough, just a few weeks prior to my attack, a young man met my mother for some informal counseling sessions. As a result, he had my mother's cell number and called my Mom to inform her of my attack. God definitely has His way of sending help when it is needed. My mother worked only a few blocks away. So, upon receiving the call, she immediately left work. She hugged and kissed me, and reassured me that everything was going to be alright, and promised to follow the ambulance in her car. It was comforting to see my mom. She stayed with me until the ambulance started on the way to the hospital.

Although I was reciting Psalm 91 internally, I needed the fortitude of a prayer warrior, so I asked the EMT if I could use her phone to call my pastor since I did not have my cell phone. Fortunately, the EMT agreed to let me use her phone, but warned me that her battery was going to go dead any second. However, I was not sure that I would remember the correct number under such a stressful condition. So I quickly dialed the number that came to my mind. Praise God, it was the correct number and the pastor answered the phone. I told her I was attacked and was being transported to the hospital as we spoke. Instantly, she started to pray. She is an avid prayer warrior and has good discernment. My pastor bathed me in prayer. Amazingly, the power in the cell phone battery only lasted until she finished praying and told me that she would meet me at the hospital.

I breathed a sigh of relief and thanked God for his mercy. I closed my eyes, hoping to catch a nap and forget about the events that transpired earlier that evening. Fearing that I would drift into a coma, the EMT would not allow me to sleep. She kept asking me questions to keep me awake.

Later, I arrived at the emergency room. As I waited, the symptoms of the trauma persisted. I cried out in anguish for the Lord to help me. It was then that I realized that I had wet my pants. The humiliation of wetting my pants as an adult made me cry even more.

Trembling with shock, I folded my arms across my chest, in an attempt to comfort myself, as I rocked back and forth crying. I needed a friend. I knew God was with me, but I felt alone. I quietly prayed that my mom and pastor would get to the hospital quickly. As I waited, I kept on calling on the Lord to deliver me. Finally the nurse came and triaged me and took me to the Radiology Department to complete X-rays and CAT scans. My thumb needed immediate medical attention, it was still bleeding profusely.

During the knife struggle, I had received a laceration. If the cut was just a fraction deeper I would have lost my thumb. Afterwards, I was transported from radiology and placed in another room, where I waited for the surgeon to repair my thumb. The wait felt like eternity. Still crying from the shock of the attack, two nurses came in to check on me. When one saw me crying, in disgust she said;

"Honey calm down. You are safe."

I was appalled at her level of insensitivity. I thought to myself;

"How would you like to experience what just happened to me? I was almost murdered!"

Totally oblivious to my plight, both nurses left me alone in the room for long time. It was terrible. None of the standard hospital procedures were followed in my case. In fact, since I was the victim of a violent attack, a crisis counselor should have been present to initiate counseling.

Fortunately for me, my mom and pastor arrived shortly after and were able to closely supervise my care and strengthen me with their love and moral support. While they were with me, the surgeon came stitched and bandaged up my thumb and then prescribed pain medication to be filled at the pharmacy. He advised me to follow up with my primary physician or return to the hospital within a few days. In the physician's assessment, my prognosis was good, so he discharged me. However, I was perplexed, and could not understand how the physician could not see that my body was still very tense. Why would he send me home without an injection to ease the tension I was still experiencing?

Upon my discharge, my mother took me home. I went to bed wanting to sleep for several days but the reality of restlessness was evident that night. It was beyond anything I had ever experienced. Although I was tired, I twisted and turned in bed all night. I could not sleep. My mind replayed the entire attack all night long. The following morning, I felt exhausted.

Waking up the next morning, I faced a new set of challenges. I discovered the extent of my injuries. Blood clots were formed in more than eighty percent of my eyes. My throat was bruised and swollen with black welts from the impressions of the attacker's fingerprints around my neck. The swelling of my neck made it difficult to speak or eat without experiencing excruciating pain. I discovered bruises on my arms, legs and other parts of my body. My chest and ribs felt contused and I ached all over my body. Even my breathing was compromised. Extreme fatigue and heaviness from a persisting headache made me feel like I had a massive concussion. Movement was almost impossible without pain. I felt like I was recovering from being badly beaten. The road to recovery seemed like it was going to be a long one. My physical injuries were greater than I thought. It was evident that my care in the emergency room was just the beginning of my medical care. Over the next several weeks, I had a series of CAT Scans, MRIs, X-rays, blood work and other diagnostic tests that were conducted to determine the type of care I needed.

As I worked with my physician on a treatment program to regain physical wellness, my mental health was of equal concern. So on my follow-up visit to the hospital, the nurse practitioner recommended immediate counseling with the director of the women's group, Safe and Sound.

Counseling turned out to be more of a blessing than I initially thought it would be at that time. The counseling sessions helped me to understand the symptoms I was experiencing and how they were related to trauma. It also helped me to process, assess and record my daily journey which led to my wellness. After the attack, counseling at Safe and Sound, offered safety and security as I moved forward. The sessions helped me to open up and begin the deep inner healing I needed.

Through counseling, I became involved in the Safe and Sound's monthly women's meetings where I met other women who had gone through violent crimes. In this place, we all come together to offer support, love and encouragement to one another on the road to recovery. The story behind each woman's life was unbelievable. Yet, so was the hurt, pain and suffering each woman experienced as she struggled to carry out her roles in life as a spouse, parent, worker, student, entrepreneur and caregiver.

The dynamics of the group allowed women in the group to share intimate details of their lives with one another. The friendships formed were rooted in the commonality of sisterhood and trauma. Nevertheless, hope and strength arose. I was amazed at the deep human connection that was formed when one person was willing and was able to share another's pain. As I became a part of the group, a new sensitivity flooded my consciousness. I became more aware of the trauma many abused women experience. Violent crimes perpetrated against women, did not discriminate against any special group or ethnicity.

Through that experience, I became informed about the demon of domestic violence. I have also seen the brokenness, shallowness and emptiness in the lives of many men in our communities. They are our coworkers, neighbors, cousins, uncles, brothers, fathers, husbands and friends who have become lost, twisted and demented in their roles as men.

A man is considered by God's standard to be the protector and preserver of a woman. The statistics in regards to violent crimes against women is much higher than we would ordinarily believe and the abuse had crossed every social, racial, academic and economic barrier. Our communities are filled with hurting men, because only a hurting person inflicts hurt on another person. I began feeling a deeper sense of obligation to be proactive by utilizing my sphere of influence to dialogue about violence that was unleashed towards women. Frequently, I held discussions with my friends, family, coworkers, students and others in the community about the seriousness of this epidemic that had infested our society.

I began to view violent behavior at work in a different way. Teaching in a high school, it was not uncommon to see students involved in rough play. Sometimes boys would body slam girls against lockers or pin them on the wall and sometimes hit them. Since the attack, these actions became magnified in my sight. Now it infuriated me. I found myself taking those young people aside and warning them of the danger in allowing themselves to become desensitized to the horrors of abuse. In pure adolescent innocence they would sometimes laugh and say,

"We are just playing."

Still, I would scold them and explain that there is nothing humorous about the portrayal of violence. This is not the type of prank to practice, because this is a daunting reality for many women. I found myself teaching young men that there role as a man is more honorable, protecting the weaker vessel, as opposed to inflicting harm. In fact, this is a part of the creation plan that God intended for mankind.

I educated each young man with a goal in mind. I believe that every boy that understands and makes a conscious decision not to become abusive has contributed towards the building of one more healthy, happy and productive family.

This would eventually lead to less incidents of violence in our communities.

A few days after the attack, the detective that had been assigned to my case asked me to go to the police station to identify the suspect and make an official report of the attack against me. As I sat in the detective's office and recollected the incident and gave my statement, I experienced a new appreciation of the miracle that occurred, despite the trauma. The detective agreed that I was lucky to be alive. After identifying the suspect from a photo, I was also asked to identify the knife used in the attack. I stared at the knife, and then looked away in disbelief as to how fortunate I was when the knife broke in two. In that moment, I looked up, and my eyes met the verse on the wall of the detective's office printed in bold letters. It was Isaiah 54:17. It stated;

"No weapons formed against me shall prosper."

I praised God because that was truly a Word from the Lord for me. The knife that was formed against me did not prosper. It broke in two!

In the meeting with the detective, extra photographs were taken, in addition to the ones taken in the emergency room. I also became very concerned about the suspect's whereabouts, including whether or not he would make bail and be back on the street. It was at that time; I was informed that the attacker was caught moments after he attacked me. In fact, I was told that when the property manager saw the attacker running from the building, he had wanted to confront him about the items the attacker had stolen from the property. So, he started chasing OW. In hot pursuit of the attacker, the property manager called the police. Responding promptly to the call, the police chased the attacker approximately five blocks from where I lived to another young woman's apartment, where he also assaulted the woman to gain entry into her apartment and hid in an attempt to escape arrest.

While the attacker was hiding in the young woman's apartment, the police came and arrested him within minutes of the first attack. The suspect was taken to the County Jail where he awaited trial for at least seven serious charges that had been brought against him.

Chapter 3

°∞°∞°∞°∞°∞°∞°∞°∞°

Surviving Trauma

Going through the ordeal of a vicious attack left physical scars, as well as leashed a venom of psychological and emotional wounds. For weeks I had red blood-shot eyes which resulted from the rupturing of blood vessels in the strangulation attempt. So every time I looked in the mirror, my eyes were a constant reminder as to how close I came to death. In fact, the popping of the eyes is one of the indicators homicide detectives use to identify strangled victims. Over and over again, as I stood before the mirror, I looked at myself in disbelief. Yet at the same time, I stood in awe of God. I was a breathing miracle! The enemy of my soul said yes to my demise, but God said no! Mercy said, "I am never going to let her go!"

My eyes made me look like an alien creature from another planet. I looked like I belonged in a science fiction movie. When I had to be in public without my dark glasses, I would hear the gasps and see the alarming facial expressions as people would stare at me or look away. Some verbalized how scary I looked, while others would try to find out if my eyes hurt or if I had blurred vision. My friend Shirley visited me three weeks after the attack and she later confessed that she had to shorten her visit because it was too difficult for her to look at me and see the horrific effects of the attack. She said even though I described it to her over the phone, it was nothing compared to seeing me in person.

Although my eyes told their own story, I was also dealing with the incapacitation of my dominant hand. During the knife fight, my thumb was cut adjacent to the first joint. Subsequently the tendon that facilitates movement of the joint had been cut. Unfortunately, when I was taken to the emergency room, the doctor that stitched up my thumb failed to reattach the tendon. So, by the time my thumb healed, I had no movement of that joint.

One cannot begin to imagine how significant the thumb is in fine motor movements. Although I studied this in anatomy, the reality was devastating. At times, I became frustrated from my inability to competently perform basic functional tasks. This was extremely difficult for me at first, because I am a young, independent, healthy and athletic woman that became somewhat disabled. Interestingly enough, although I knew it would not hinder my life from going forward, I remember feeling such a great loss. In fact, the loss was magnified one hundred times in my mind. By losing the use of my hand, I suddenly realized the limitations on grasping as well as other hand movements. I also grieved the loss of learning to play the piano. This, in particular, made me sad because I was looking forward to taking piano lessons again.

As I mourned inwardly, I had to come to a point where I realized that God spared my life and that alone was significant. The partial functional loss of one of my thumbs is not the same as losing a thumb. Besides, I could have lost my finger. However, this was not the case. I had to gain proper perspective. This brought me to another level of trusting God to get through this part of the trauma. I also decided I was going to be joyous in my heart and praise God despite my circumstances. As I started focusing on God, instead of my thumb, He supernaturally changed my perspective, by renewing my mind in His Word. By Him doing this, I no longer mourned my loss like a person without hope.

For several weeks, I suffered from extreme weakness and fatigue. It is amazing how the fight for my life took not only courage but much strength. My body felt like it was literally broken down and needed to be rebuilt again. I was quite exhausted and I often felt like I had no strength. In fact, I remember thinking that if I had to go through this ordeal again I would not be strong enough to survive it. Then the Lord reminded me that I was made strong through Him in my weakness. Besides, He was the one that was keeping me. He was the one that was my Protector. Truly, He is the one that saved my life from destruction.

The low energy levels I experienced affected my ability to drive and carry out routine tasks. As a result, I had no choice but to call on God's Word more and see His power manifest itself in a greater way. As I prayed, I quoted verses out loud such as Psalm 121:1, which states;

"I will lift my eyes to the hill from whence cometh my help. My help comes from the Lord who made heaven and earth."

I literally had to hold on to God's Word and trust in the Lord for strength to get through the day. I had to understand that the Lord is my strength and Redeemer. Therefore, when fear and frustration from my weakness tried to creep in my mind I had to remember that because my strength is from the Lord; there was nothing I had to fear. In other words, there was no situation that arises that God is not able to handle on my behalf. This is especially true when I put my trust in Him. As I look back on this difficult time, I praise the Lord for teaching me His Word experientially. This often caused me to say;

"Now I have seen God's words in the Bible take life and do what He said they would do."

This was such an awesome thing to witness. It stirred up my faith in God to see His demonstrative power.

As time passed, I started regaining more of my physical strength and the battle scars became less obvious. People frequently asked how I was doing and would often times commend me on how great I looked. Initially, I would have a hard time accepting compliments because I was feeling horrible. So, I would often say;

"My wounds are deeper than what meets the eye."

I did not want to ignore how bad I felt by masking the snares from the incident. For several weeks, I would try to dress in a way that would deter attention. Prior to the attack, I did not seek attention through my attire. Interestingly enough, after the attack, I became preoccupied about not wanting to be noticed. So, I intentionally tried to appear less attractive. I would also reject the idea completely if a man found me attractive, and become extremely irritable if a man showed any type of interest in me. I just could not process the idea of someone loving me in the condition I was in. There were several times, I would literally run away from men if they showed the slightest amount of interest.

Sometimes I just wanted the earth to open up and take me in. I was an emotional shell. There were times when I felt the enemy was going to succeed in killing me. This was even compounded by the fact that days after the attack, there was an attempted forced entry into my apartment. I never had such an experience. It was one of the worst feelings. I felt I was being hunted like a dog. I was fearful at times and I cried a lot. I felt alone.

The burden of dealing with the police, lawyers, doctors and counselors involved in the case was overwhelming. Prior to the incident, I lived a fairly full life and maintained a busy schedule. Adding more meetings to my schedule while I had a fragile state of mind was not easy for me. I felt so weak and mentally incapable of moving ahead. Nevertheless, I trusted in God to deliver me. There were days that I was so spiritually depleted, I could not pray for myself, but I thank God for having a prayer group with people that prayed for me during this period.

Joy Payne Phillips was very instrumental during this time as she faithfully bathed me in prayer. When she prays the dead rise, so I knew all fear, uncertainty and satanic devices had to eventually flee. My story is proof that prayer works! Only prayer could have gotten me through this time. God answers prayers. God's Word states;

"The effectual and fervent prayers of the righteous avail much." -James 5:16

Worship was another fundamental Christian practice that helped me to overcome the attack. Our lives ought to be lifestyles of worship, which is our reasonable form of praise unto God. Yet, it is in the moments when I set aside an appointed time just to serenade God and lay prostrate before God Almighty that I receive the greatest infilling from God. It is not just an expression to say;

"When the praises go up, the blessings come down."

But it is truth! Worship lifts God Almighty up. It honors and adores him. Worship lavishes the praise and glory of God. This pleases the Father and subsequently evokes his presence.

The Bible clearly says in the presence of the Lord there is fullness of joy and pleasures at his right hand forever more. There is a fulfillment and ultimate satisfaction in blessing the Name of the Lord in worship. Understanding this revolutionized my thinking and overall attitude going through the trial. Worship was my secret weapon, which is sharper than any two edged sword. Used in the right context, it creates such an upset in the enemy's camp that one becomes untouchable. In worship, we become truly untouchable by life's circumstances! Radical worship in the midst of tribulation shapes character, which helps us to graduate to the next level of our destiny, because God had tried us and we are now approved. It is important to worship God through the trials in our life, and watch God promote us to the next level or help us to overcome difficult circumstances.

In my own situation, the attack occurred on a Friday and so that following Sunday, I knew I had to be in church. Feeling the sting of the physical, emotional and psychological trauma, my inner man yearned to be in God's house. There was a cry lingering in the depths of my soul. There was unrest. I had to find rest. God bids those of us who are heavy laden to come to Him. We should go and continue going to Him, because he promises to give us rest. His burden is light and his yoke is easy. So I ran to the house of the Lord, to cast my cares on Him. I needed God more than ever! I was so broken, overwhelmed and stricken to the core of my soul. I had to worship God Almighty in His house. It did not matter how my body was doing physically, because I knew that once my spirit man was robust, I could overcome anything!

So, I pressed my way to service that Sunday morning and received much deliverance, especially when the pastor asked me to lead worship that morning. There was a praise that stirred up in my belly and flowed out of my being as if God himself was worshiping through me. It was the type of worship I called an 'open heaven experience.' The Spirit of God filled that church as I worshipped God. At that point, it was not about leading a congregation in worship, but it was about tapping into the heavens, glorifying God for my life and getting what valium could not offer an ailing soul. As I worshipped God, a shofaristic sound of resounding victory came forth. Death tried to swallow me up in the grave. But I could stand and sing;

"Oh death, where is your sting? Oh Hades where is your victory?" -1 Cor. 15:55

By the power of the Lamb of God, Jesus first overcame death, so I defied death. So, for a combination of reasons, I could not allow anything or anyone to contain my praise. In worship, I was going to get all I needed to go on. I remember, talking with a group of women from my monthly prayer meeting and they were so impressed with my strength and zeal for the Lord when I told them that I went to church the Sunday after the attack. But I knew and God knew that I had to! Even when I did not feel like it, I had to speak to myself. In fact, l had to lay hands on my chest and say to myself, as David the Psalmist did.

"Why are you so down cast in me, O my soul? Why are you so disquieted in me? Hope in God. For I shall yet praise Him." -Psalm 43:5

This truly was not about my tenacity, but a mere need I had, and I recognized God was the source I needed to fill that void!

By the grace of God I never had any cognitive deficits, but the trauma caused me to momentarily forget my schedule. This was probably one the most frightening symptoms that manifested from the attack. For a few weeks, I had difficulty remembering at times what I was supposed to be doing and when I was supposed to be doing it. This manifested itself in lesser extremes when I was home for a while, but when I went back to work I had difficulty remembering my schedule. I felt like a fish out of water. I almost had to become re-acclimated with my classes, the curriculum and almost everything else that related to work. It was actually a blessing to have the love and support of my supervisor and co-workers who were instrumental in helping me through this period.

Interestingly, many people did not realize my daily struggle, unless I said something about my condition. Instead, many have said privately and openly that they are surprised at how well I was doing. Again, I thought that my wounds were beneath the skin. But in retrospect, it was the grace of God on my life that had helped me to be and do all that I needed to do under such high stress levels. In fact, grace is supernatural empowerment to accomplish anything. So it was

God's sustaining power that kept me even when I did not know what I should be doing. The Holy Spirit guided me, since God promised that His Spirit would lead us into all truth. It was also my comforter when I needed assurance that I could conquer the incident.

I was continuously reminded that as a Born Again Believer, I have embraced Jesus Christ as my personal Savior, repented and accepted that he died for my sins on the cross at Calvary. So, by acceptance of Christ, I am a Child of God and because of this, Christ is living on the inside of me. The Word of God states;

"He who is in you is greater than he who is in the world." -1 John 4:4b

Therefore, having the presence of God residing in me, gives me the ability to be a conqueror. The scripture state;

"I can do all things through Christ who strengthens me." -Philippians 4:13

This is the key to overcoming! Haphazardly, recounting scriptures is not good enough, but we must pray, meditate, reflect, ponder and think upon the scriptures, allowing them to get into our being; renew our minds, and in turn influence our actions.

Chapter 4

°∞°∞°∞°∞°∞°∞°∞°∞°

The Trial

Several weeks had passed. I continued with my medical treatments and counseling sessions. I also met frequently with the prosecutor to receive updates on the status of the case. The process was tedious, but I was determined not to be overwhelmed by this stressful ordeal. Although frustrated at times with the lengthy, meandering process of our justice system, I relied on my faith, which gave me hope to believe that the trial would quickly come to an end. In fact, within a few months of the attack, there was the grand jury trial. As the time approached, the prosecutor briefed me on what I could expect and repeatedly gave me the option of not testifying if reliving the trauma was too psychologically stressful for me. I never wanted to relive that trauma again, but I understood that no one, but me could tell my story. Besides, I felt that it was my civic duty to testify as a citizen of my community. I also believed that I represented the voice of many women in similar circumstances that were silenced by death or intimidation from potential retaliation.

I told the prosecutor that;

> "I am the voice of every, child, teenager, young, middle-aged and elderly woman that could have been going home that day. I must testify. I will not allow fear to prevent me from doing my part in protecting the innocent from this savage."

The prosecutor commended me and said;

> "Very well. So you will testify, but if you change your mind at anytime, let me know and I will remove the plug."

I agreed. However, there was no changing my mind. That's it! When I make up my mind about something, there is no turning back. I am often accused of being stubborn. In this case, testifying was a minimal cost. As a matter of fact, testifying was not a huge price to pay if it would lead to a safer community.

The grand jury date was set for a Monday morning at nine o' clock. The night before the grand jury, was the first time since the attack that I allowed my mind to replay the full incident from beginning to end. It was extremely difficult, because I had compartmentalized the incident in an effort to move on with my life. In any case, I had to visit memory lane if I was going to testify the following morning.

As I prepared for court that morning, I prayed that God would allow me to experience his peace while I clearly and fluidly articulated the precise occurrence of the events surrounding the attack. I was a little nervous, but after I prayed I had a reassuring confidence that God was with me. One of my girlfriends, Keesh, accompanied me to court. We were later joined in court by the Director of Human Resources for the School District I was employed. I never had any court dealings of this nature before, so this was very new to me. The moral support from my friends eased the nervous tension. In fact, my closest encounter with court matters was limited to watching court trials on TV.

Looking at my summons to appear in court that morning, I double checked the room number on the door before entering a medium sized, grey toned and bland room, with chairs arranged in untidy rows. Although it was only 8:30 A. M. the room seemed to be fairly crowded. I handed my slip to a Caucasian gentleman who was dressed in civilian clothing that was sitting by the door. I believe that he was a police officer because he had a displayed gun and badge. He quickly glanced over my summons, and beckoned me to have a seat until my name was called. He said that I would be directed into another room where I would testify. My friend and I scanned the room to find a comfortable and non-intrusive area that would afford us some privacy to talk while we waited. We found a spot, and settled in two old uncomfortable chairs.

As we waited, I looked around the room at the people and could not help but wonder what events brought them here... murder charges, rape, robbery, drug... and what roles would they play in these cases. As I looked at the faces around the room, I was reminded that these were ordinary people. I imagined each person had an extraordinary story and we were all linked together by the role we had to play in the justice system that morning.

Occasionally, I checked my watch and engaging in small talk with my friends, my name was finally called. I was motioned into another private room, where I stood before a group of men and women seated in a semicircle that filled the span of the room. The walls of the room were cherry oak stained in color, plain in appearance and poorly lit. There were no decorative paintings or obvious style to the décor of the room. The American flag was lowered in one corner. In the middle, there was an empty desk and chair with a microphone projected from the desk. I imagined I would be sitting. Just a few feet over was the court recorder, already in position and she was typing away at a record breaking speed. I was always impressed with the speed at which these people typed.

Furthermore, at the beginning of the semicircle, I spotted the prosecutor, who nodded and half smiled, upon my entrance into the room. On the prosecutor's left, there was another middle-aged bald gentleman who seemed to be leading the proceedings. I don't remember who he was, but I concluded that he must have been the judge. The other twelve people in the circle were the jurors. At that moment all eyes were on me. I felt like the spotlight was turned on me. I was asked to sit at the empty desk, speak clearly and loudly into the microphone and state my name for the record. I did, and then the prosecutor asked several questions. First, she verified the location in which the incident occurred. Later, I was asked to describe the events that transpired on September 14, 2007.

Briefly I paused to gather my thoughts. I sighed, looked across the room and then allowed my stare to focus on the prosecutor. Calmly, I started rehashing the events leading up to my attack on that day. Maintaining composure, I started to vividly describe moment by moment the grueling attack and how the attacker pinned me on the floor of my apartment and pressed the knife blade against my throat. I attempted to give every detail so I could create a clear picture of the experience to ensure that the men and women of the court had sufficient information to determine what had occurred.

As I spoke, I felt like I had stepped into the scene of the attack and I was experiencing it again. I described how I saw my life flashing before my eyes and thought I was going to die. Emphatically I said;

"I am too young to die."

Overcome with the reality of the incident during my testimony, the emotional trauma became paramount, as I testified. I shook my head,

"No! No! No!"

I broke down in tears and wept bitterly. I am not sure how long I cried, but the court secretary had to stop the recording. I sobbed bitterly in my hands, as the jury watched me relive the trauma. They graciously gave me time to bury the emotional anguish of my soul into my hands. After some time had passed, someone cautiously, asked if I would like to continue as someone handed me a tissue to wipe my tears and offered me water to drink. In a small voice I responded,

"Yes. I just need a moment."

I drank some more water, took a deep breath, dried my face, regained my composure and continued sharing the rest of the story. Upon finishing my story, some of the members of the jury had a few questions for me. One of the questions included how I was able to identify the attacker if he had a mask on his face. I answered the question by explaining that the wide eye holes in the mask made it easy to recognize his face by his complexion and skeletal facial features. Besides, I also recognized his voice. When all questions and concerns were satisfied, I was thanked for coming and was dismissed from the room.

Arising from the chair, I breathed a sigh of relief, straightened my suit and walked out of the room. As I exited the room, I felt an overwhelming peace that flooded my soul. I literally felt the Holy Spirit hugging me in a comforting way. Stepping through the door, I exhaled, thanked God for his mercies and went to join my friends who were waiting for me in the waiting area. One step closer to resolving this matter, I informed my friends about the events that transpired during the grand jury meeting. Later, we gathered our things and left the court building.

Approximately three weeks had passed since the grand jury meeting had taken place. It was decided that the defendant was not going to be charged with attempted murder, but instead with first degree aggravated assault, among six other charges. Besides going through the attack, this was the worst news I had heard concerning the trial. I could not understand how it was possible that the court could not see that he was trying to kill me. He practically tried to strangle me. I was disgusted and disappointed in the court system and felt that because he did not succeed in killing me, charging the defendant for murder was less justifiable. Outraged about the judicial system, again I had to lean heavily on God to give me even greater peace to accept the outcome. So like any other concerns or burdens in my life, I had to cast that too, on Him, who cares deeply for me.

Several months had passed and while I was awaiting the trial, the trial date was frequently postponed. Delay after delay smashed my hope in believing that the trial would quickly come to an end. So, as I prayed about the court proceedings, I gained strength to endure. After some time had elapsed, the defendant consulted with his lawyer and decided to accept a plea bargain arrangement so the case did not go to trial. He pled guilty to the charges presented against him. I believe it was done in an effort to strike a deal with the prosecution for less time.

Chapter 5

°∞°∞°∞°∞°∞°∞°∞°∞°

A Purpose To Live For

In Jeremiah 29:11, God says;

"For I know the plans I have for you, to give you a future and an expected end."

This verse speaks definitively of a special purpose that God has mandated for each of our lives, even before the earth was established. He thought of us, predestined us, and who He predestines He justifies through Jesus Christ. This was a carefully designed plan to establish God's will throughout mankind. However, the pressures of life and sin have a way of causing us to feel alone and isolated from the will of God. This could cause us to find it difficult to believe that the God of heaven and earth has a divine plan for our lives. The enemy wants us to believe we are insignificant and God does not really care about the details of our lives. Although many people agree that God cares about their lives, it is sometimes difficult for the mind to conceive and accept the love of God. Often, this difficulty is a stronghold in the mind and needs to be broken.

God wants to accomplish great things with our lives. So as we read the Word of God, we must pray that it renews our minds so that our thinking will line up with His thoughts. Then our actions will be God focused and purpose oriented. God's purpose for our lives is simple. Walking in God's purpose makes our lives worth living. I have also realized that life's struggles, failures, disappointments and circumstances can frequently lead us into a place of fear and complacency where we stop striving towards fulfilling the plan we were created to accomplish. The hardships of life may cause you to lose sight of the goal God has placed in your heart or your passion may wane for the same dream that once kept you up in the middle of the night. When this occurs, our purpose can be derailed, and even become extinct when time-sensitive missions are missed in there appointed seasons.

However, a passion for God's Kingdom to come and His will done in the earth realm are catalysts behind one's urgency to fulfill the call of God. Another fueling factor is the eminence of death. As in my case, when I came face to face with death, it caused me to appreciate the fragility of life and realize that life is very uncertain. We can be here today and gone tomorrow. We are like grass, the wind blows and its' place is remembered no more. That is why the Bible states that we should take no concern for tomorrow because it is not promised to any of us. Nevertheless, we have a hope in Christ Jesus!

In Psalm 91, we see that if we set our affections on the Lord, He delivers us, honors us and satisfies us with long life. Repeatedly, God promises to uphold the righteous but cut off the wicked! Because I am redeemed by God and I am called righteous, God saved my life from destruction. Death is not a respecter of persons. The enemy is serious about fulfilling his mission. He does not discriminate between old and young.

"The thief does not come except to steal, and to kill and to destroy." -John 10:10

He does not play fair. He is the devourer. So we must be diligent about pursuing God's business, at all costs!

As I went to the precipice of death and back to life, this encounter had turned me upside down. I was changed. I had a new mindset. I had always been tenacious. Now, there was a difference about my tenacity. There was a brokenness in my spirit that had caused me to give up my own agendas. I wanted God's Will even more for my life. I realized that time was limited and I must hurry to perform the things that God had commissioned me to do.

Now I hear the clock ticking like never before. So, I am compelled to act swiftly. Not out of trepidation but out of spiritual revelation and understanding. The same goes for you, don't allow circumstances to hinder you from fulfilling God's plan for your life. It is time. Stop second guessing yourself and act accordingly!

One of my favorite Psalms is Psalm103, which states;

"Bless the Lord oh my soul and forget not his benefits, who redeems my life from destruction."
-Psalms 103:1&4

If I did not know before the attack, I now know beyond a shadow of a doubt that God saved me from death for a purpose. In fact, He snatched me out of the jaws of death! It encouraged my faith and prayer life to see the scriptures coming to life on my behalf actively doing what God said it would accomplish. Just imagine God Almighty, gave his angels charge over me that day to keep my life in all ways. This was evident when the attacker first tried to rape me and did not succeed. Then he tried to cut my throat but God prevented that tragedy by allowing the blade to be separated from the handle and he could not find it! Then later, the man attempted to strangle me until I passed out and he thought I was dead. Again, God revived me within moments. The enemy would want me to ponder, oh God why me? And perhaps agonize over how God could possibly allow this to happen. Or probably question the significance of the purpose God created for my life. However, throughout the process, I thank God for divine empowerment which caused me to put aside such divisive thinking.

As I journey in Christ, I have come to understand that;

"All things work together for good to those who love the Lord and are called according to his purpose." -Romans 8:28.

And this included me! I love the Lord and I am called by Him. I am his workmanship, created for good works in Christ Jesus. So are you! Subsequently, God is able to use everything in our lives for His glory. The very thing that the enemy intended for evil, God has the amazing capacity to reverse it for our good and His glory. That is why He is known as the restorer, redeemer and repairer of the breech. Only God Almighty can bring forth life out of death. He uses the very thing intended to kill one to generate life. Imagine how great our God is! Even in the storms of death, heartbreaks, losses and disappointments; God uses these things to demonstrate His wonderful working power, for His Name sake.

Keeping in mind, His ultimate plan for our lives is to prosper us, I refuse to believe or accept anything contrary to the original plan God has for my life. Full assurance in my heart helps me to believe that God will not abort nor frustrate his purpose for our lives, because He who started a good work is faithful to bring it to completion. That is why God is known as the author and finisher of our faith. In other words, God will do what He says He will do. He stands by His word!

Chapter 6

°∞°∞°∞°∞°∞°∞°∞°∞°

Leaving the Past Behind

Paul was a man that had tremendous accomplishments in the Christian faith when he wrote this verse under the inspiration of the Holy Spirit.

> "I press towards the mark of the high calling in Christ Jesus, forgetting that which is behind." -Philippians 3:14

Although Paul had written much of the New Testament and successfully evangelized the Gospel of Christ to people all over the world, among other accomplishments, Paul realized that as commendable as these things were, there was still a lot of work to be done for God's kingdom. Therefore, he could not live in the past. Paul understood that God's mercies are new every morning and God is continuously doing a new thing. We cannot press forward in the things of God if we continue to look at our pasts. If we keep looking back, we will never move forward. This is such a simple concept with a profound impact. We must not allow our minds or thoughts to be fixated on past accomplishments or failures, or else we will never attain the fullness of God's plan for our lives.

Following Paul, as he follows Christ, we should pattern our lives in this order. All of us have a past! Well, for some it is probably more tainted than others, but nevertheless, we have all had some unpleasant experiences or trauma that we have had to deal with. Sometimes life circumstances cut into the core of our being. It causes us to experience anger, hurt, deep pain, bitterness, failure and frustration, along with other deep emotional expressions that the enemy uses to keep us in a state of condemnation. Many of you know the voices that seem to speak so loudly in our ears. Those voices try to drown out the Word of God. God says there is no condemnation to those who are in Christ.

In other words, if you put your trust in the Lord and you are pressing to uphold his statutes, you are one of His own. He has redeemed you with His shed blood on Calvary. He has forgiven you. When God looks at us, He does not see the blemishes from our past nor does He see our mistakes nor the mishaps, tragedies and the losses. He sees us in our redeemed state, full of life, potential and possibilities that are to be utilized for His glory. The problem lies within our minds. The enemy knows this and makes this a battle zone that is worst than many war zones. It is in our minds our purposes often die because we feel defeated, which in turn causes us to remain stuck in our past. Imagine that! Satan uses our minds to carry out his agenda! One of the ways he does this is by replaying in our minds the distressing events that occurred in our lives and the hurtful words spoken to us. It is as if he has a DVD of the condemning scenes of our lives that he plays repeatedly with every given opportunity. Just when we seem to be moving on from our past that is the time he hits the play button on the remote control of our past. This frequently cripples many from pursuing their purposes.

Others are haunted by nightmares of the past which permanently immobilize them. This is deeper than just someone saying, "Get over this!" or "Just move on!" The Holy Spirit truly has to intervene and psychologically rehabilitate one's mind so that they may think properly. This entails God renewing our minds through His Word in conjunction with practical steps we must incorporate in our lives to keep our minds healthy.

Understanding the importance of leaving the past behind is critical in embracing new beginnings. In regards to my story, the incident I endured had caused several nightmares, long after the attack. I became so sensitive to my surroundings. I heard every sound. If a leaf rustled I heard it. Just a startling sound would cause me to relive the experience. It was horrific. My body would go through the physiological effects as if I were being attacked again. My heart would palpitate as my chest tightened and my upper body would become tense. At the same time my hands would lock into tightly clenched fists. Sometimes, I was overcome with shock and fear and I would scream;

"No!"

Later, I was reminded that it was just an image from my past. The first time I drove after the attack, I remember pulling along the side of the road to verify some driving directions on a fairly busy roadway and I had my head down. Unbeknownst to me, another car pulled up behind my car and a tall gentleman dressed in black got out of the car. I looked up, I saw him right by the driver's door of my car. I was so frightened. I almost wet my pants. My body convoluted with fear and many other accompanying emotions I experienced since the attack came. I could not believe what was happening to me. My heart was racing rapidly and my head was pounding. I felt like I was going to die. Bracing myself, I looked at the gentleman again and he was not on the driver's side of the car, in fact, he was passing by the passenger side of the car, on his way into an adjacent building.

When I realized he was not coming to attack me, I thanked God and broke down crying. I became a victim of my imagination. I survived the trauma physically but I was just a mere shell. God had to deliver me. I could not go around fearing every tall Black man I saw. I wept bitterly because I became a fragile and fearful woman. I did not like it. It was like watching a fearful frightened woman, stricken with grief, and I could do nothing about it, because that woman was me. I felt powerless. I began to realize the gravity of the stronghold that was trying to grip me in its claws. I did not want to become a woman that would be afraid of men, nor did I want to develop unhealthy phobias of men that were stereotypical judgments I had conjured in my mind about colored men. Up to that point of my life, I had a fairly healthy outlook and relationship with the opposite gender. I wanted it to remain that way and not be inhibited by the offense of one twisted Black man. I needed prayer!

Something in my soul was broken and I needed the Holy Spirit to fix it! I have too much to accomplish for God with my life to be hindered by my perception. As I sat in my car, I prayed silently;

"Dear Jesus, Help me overcome this. Do not let this incident cripple my life."

I later shared the experience with my prayer group and close friends who lifted me up in prayer. However, at times when I had to take the elevator or be in an enclosed area with another man, I would see him as a potential attacker. I would become extremely guarded. Externally I do my best to remain composed, but internally, I was falling apart. Many times, I felt that everyone saw right through me. In these moments, I would encourage myself with the scriptures.

"I am more that a conqueror in Christ."
-Philippian4:13

"Yeah though I walk through the valley of death, I will fear no evil, for thou art with me, thy rod and staff comfort me."
-Psalm 23:4

"Fear not, I will never leave you nor forsake you." -Hebrews 13:5

"The Lord is my light and my salvation;
Whom shall I fear?
The Lord is the strength of my life;
Of whom shall I be afraid" –Psalm 27:1

"Though an army may encamp against me,
My heart will not fear..." –Psalm 27:3

As I battled the fear of another attack, the more I had to pray God's Word and lean on His strength.

My past would also plague me at bedtime. The moment I laid down, the video tape of the incident would play. I suffered from vivid flashbacks of the attacker straddling my body and squeezing my neck into a lifeless loll in a recurring nightmare. Again, I relived the symptoms of the attack, both in my body and mind. Sometimes it seemed like the harder I tried to get it out of my mind, the more persistent the imagery replay would be. This would interrupt my sleep for a couple hours each night. I cried out to the Lord to deliver me because I could not become dependent on prescription drugs to replenish the body's natural equilibrium. The mind of the righteous is blessed. So, I pleaded the blood of Jesus over my thoughts and my subconscious when I went to sleep. I also became more mindful of what I watched and listened to prior to bedtime, because it was not uncommon for me to watch the news before I slept. And you know as well as I do, the ten and eleven o'clock news programs are riddled with some of the most violent and heinous crimes, which were just like my attack. Sometimes the only difference was I survived. So, I can talk and write about it. For several weeks after the attack, I could not watch the news nor certain TV programs, especially detective and forensic type movies. Frequently, the graphic display of such films was too much of a fresh reminder for me. I felt it was like watching my story on film.

So I tried to keep my mind in a state of worship prior to bedtime, by reading the Bible, listening to worship music or praying. These practices cultivated the presence of the Lord, which brought an inner peace and created an atmosphere conducive to sweet rest. As I implemented this antidote, my restless nights became an old story of the past. See, we can impact our spirit through our mind by what we feed our eye and ear gates. These are also conduits to past experiences that the enemy can use to torment. Therefore, monitoring my gateways enabled me to put the past behind. As time went on, the strength of the grip of the past loosened and over time, I began to experience a breakthrough.

The fear of unlocked doors was probably by far the greatest fear I had to overcome, and the one that took me the longest to break free from. Even now, I still have times where the residual effect of the attack concerning doors surfaces. However, when it does, I just continue casting that care on the Lord. I almost became obsessive with checking and rechecking the doors to make sure that they were secured at all times. In fact, I had developed a routine when I go home. While I parked my car, I constantly scoped out my surroundings, always double checking to make sure no undesirables were in sight. Then I would quickly exit the car with my keys ready to open the door by turning to the side, to ensure adequate visibility of my surroundings. Once clear, I would quickly open and close the door. Before I could relax and enjoy being at home, I looked around for any unusual signs. Thoroughly checking to make sure no one had been inside or that no one was currently there, waiting for me. I remember the first few times I would open up all the doors, cupboards and closets in my home. Imagine how arduous this task was, especially if you have many doors. I was paranoid for some time.

One evening I came home from work. I was exhausted after a long day and I just wanted to go straight to my bedroom and lay down, but I had to do the routine check! After checking the first few doors, I felt this overwhelming feeling that the attack was controlling my life. I could not take it anymore! I cried out in a shriek of frustration;

"God! What am I doing?"

I could not imagine going through the rest of my life checking every single door and furniture in my house, every time I entered my home. I needed deliverance to break free from the obsessive acts in trying to ensure my safety. Shortly afterwards, I had one of the most eye opening and life-changing revelations. I knew without a shadow of a doubt that it was the Holy Spirit that whispered in my ear.

"You can do all you can to be safe, but you ultimately have to trust Me to keep you safe! Despite the incident, I kept you from great tragedy."

The voice of God stopped me in my paths. I said;

"No more doors and closets routines."

So whenever, I was tempted to check the cupboards, doors, under the beds and other furniture, I have to remind myself I trust God with my life. I trust His protection, I trust Him for my safety. He is my help.

"I will look to the hill from whence cometh my help, my help cometh from the Lord who made heaven and earth" -Psalm 121:1-2

My trust in God gives the assurance referenced below in Psalm 91:5-7;

"You shall not be afraid of the terror by night. Nor for the arrow that flies by day. Nor for the pestilence in darkness. Nor for the destruction that lays waste at noonday. A thousand shall fall at your side, and ten thousand at your right hand; BUT IT SHALL NOT COME NEAR YOU!"

Several times it had been a struggle, but I had to pray, until I believed it enough to experience relief from all my fears. It worked!

Sometimes I would become startled by a shadow, or a falling object that created an unfamiliar sound. That sound would drive me into a fearful mode of being attacked again. And again, I continue to decree the creative power of God over my mind and emotions until I experience the freedom of Christ, because I refused to be held in the entrapments of the vile attack of the past. Therefore, if God did it for me, He will do it for you!

Chapter 7

°∞°∞°∞°∞°∞°∞°∞°∞°

Hope in Despair

Everyone, at some point in time feels despair when caught between a rock and a hard place; and they need a miracle from God. Desperation is the driving force that causes one to seek out alternatives to resolve the tests of life. Nonetheless, we should always consider the cost of our options, because confidence in our plans should be first grounded in God's Will. David knew this and said;

> "It is better to trust in the Lord than to put confidence in man." -Psalm 118:8

God has all the answers. Everything in creation is bare before Him. Besides God, who else is all knowing? So we must trust Him to give us insight about our desperate situations. When we understand and exercise this principle, we can boldly say that God is our hope. Those who know Christ as Lord and Savior have a hope and by faith will rely on Him regardless of life's trials.

Since the attack, I struggled to regain normalcy in my life, as I dealt with the medical attention I needed, counseling and the legal issues surrounding the trial, as well as the rumors and speculation about what occurred during the attack. Sometimes I would pass my fellow colleagues in the hallway at work, and they would whisper behind my back.

"I hope she is okay. I heard it was quite an ordeal. I am surprised she is back at work!"

The comments were endless. Some were even saying I was raped and I was in an abusive relationship that resulted in this vicious attack. The gossip was endless and added more stress to my state of despair. But I had to press even more into the things of God to encourage myself. It is never easy or pleasant to have an entire building of employees talking about you. Sometimes I thought it would be easier if they asked me what happened! Just when I thought that was bad enough, I caught my students' passing notes and whispering in class that I was raped. Again, I had to put my trust in the Lord that he would enable me to stand, go through and not be put to shame. Those who put their trust in the Lord will never be put to shame. I saw God rise up on my behalf and cover me in light of the rumors in my workplace and community. Some days were very discouraging and I could not get through the day unless I trusted in the Lord. Psalm 7:5 states;

"For you are my hope O Lord God."

Indeed, God was my hope in this darkness!

The incident also caused me to use up all my sick and personal days for the entire year at the beginning of the school year. When I realized this, I tried getting the union representative for my building to advocate on my behalf to get some additional sick days, but nothing was in place for employees dealing with a tragedy of that sort. So, after a series of meetings and phone calls, I was still left with no additional sick or personal days for the remainder of the year. At that point, there was nothing I could do. I simply had to trust God to keep me from getting sick for the remainder of the year because if I were out, I would not be paid. However, not being sick all year is a very tall order for a school teacher dealing with sick children every day. My prayer was a simple one...

"God my hope is in you. Keep me safe from sickness during the remainder of the school year."

Praise God, He did! I did not even have a common cold within the remaining nine months of the school year.

My hope in God reminds me of the scripture that highlights God's great power in us. This power is the empowerment of the Holy Spirit through Christ Jesus. He that is in us, His children, is greater than he that is in people that are not his children. We have an incredible sustaining resilience that gives us hope to believe and stand. So even if we are hard pressed on every side, we are not crushed; when perplexed, we are not in despair; and if we are struck down, we are not destroyed! This is the true inheritance of our hope in God! That is why I could trust that

God was going to help me to overcome all my struggles.

My friend, Akeem, who is a Believer, says he always wins because there is a magic in believing. This is a type of belief that does not rely on our special abilities or resources, but trusts in the confidence of a great God who causes us to triumph. In fact, I agree with Akeem because the Bible says;

> "Yet in all things we are more than conquers through Him who loved us." -Romans 8:37

If we are on Christ's team we will always be victorious. So, there is definitely a miracle that is performed in believing that God can move on our behalf in every situation. Indeed this is the basis of our hope in despair!

Chapter 8

°∞°∞°∞°∞°∞°∞°∞°∞°

Forgiveness

The true test of forgiveness occurs when someone has inflicted pain on an individual and the afflicted is able to consciously process the hurt, pain and anguish from the experience, yet deliberately chooses to pardon the offender. Regardless of the depth of the wound inflicted, this is not an easy task. As Christians, God requires that we forgive those who offend us. Not once or twice, but all the time. God even challenges us to love our enemies. Loving those that persecute us takes divine enablement. Just think about the last person that tried to harm you. Not necessarily inflicting bodily injury, but maybe you were hurt by rumors, or there was a coworker or a boss that made your work more difficult. Sometimes we are hurt due to being overlooked for a well-deserved promotion. For others it could be a vicious defamation of character which in turn limits any possible job elevation.

The list of hurts, pain, betrayal and disappointments that many of us have experienced is endless. We sometimes experience the deepest hurt from the people we love and trust such as, people that have ruled over us or those that are close to us. Hurt inflicted under any circumstance makes it difficult for many to forgive the offender or offenders. The pain can be so deeply embedded in the heart; it festers for years causing one to become bitter and cynical. I have seen relationships greatly affected by unforgiveness. An afflicted person that carries a grudge experiences more harm than the inflictor.

So forgiveness is necessary for the afflicted person's mental, emotional, physical and relational well being. God knows this and encourages us to forgive one another, just as he forgave us. Forgiveness is the foundation of the

Christian faith. If you look at what is happening in the world, you will see the wretched state of mankind. Yet, when God saw us in our sin, He had compassion and forgave us because He loved us with an everlasting love. What an awesome love? That is why in John15:13 states;

"Greater love we have not known than this, that a man would lay down his life for his friends."

Unconditional love breathes forgiveness. Those who have embraced Christ as Savior are supposed to be transformed into the likeness of Him. Part of this transformation allows us to be empowered to do as Christ did in the face of persecution. He forgave. The ultimate example of this was His journey to the cross at Calvary, when He was jeered and beaten. Yet, in the midst of his pain and suffering, he said,

"Father, forgive them, for they know not what they do!" -Luke 23:34

It is possible to forgive in the midst of hurt. Just look to Christ for courage and strength to forgive those that have wounded you. Sometimes the hurt we experience breaks our heart and God is aware of the pain and so he promises in His

Word to heal our broken hearts and bind up our wounds. There is deep inner healing in forgiveness. God truly empowers us by his grace to experience his healing touch, as well as the supernatural ability to love those that have caused us great pain.

As you have had your personal challenges with forgiving a person that has caused you pain, I have had challenges too. However, the real test of how much I would walk in the image of Christ and demonstrate forgiveness came about when I had to forgive my attacker. I was very angry at this young man because he violated me. I felt that I lived in the area long enough and had a very good rapport with everyone and had also gained the respect of my neighbors. Besides, as a worker of the building, my safety was entrusted to him. And through the wickedness of his heart, he abused the position of his authority to gain access to the vacant apartment that he came from in order to attack me. He had caused me tremendous grief. I have suffered through this attack in so many ways. I wanted him to pay for what he did to me. I wanted justice!

I was very diligent in keeping up with the prosecutor's office to ensure that they would not treat me like just any other victim and forget my case. I wanted to be remembered. Repeatedly, I emphasized to the prosecutor that everything must be done, to bring about the verdict he deserves. Initially, I became so consumed. I felt that as a citizen that survived such a brutal attack within my community, I had a responsibility to cooperate to the best of my ability and to keep this man behind bars. I represented the voice of all the women who were brutally attacked. If I were a feeble woman, I may not be here today. I felt a sense of obligation to do the right thing.

When the detective that was assigned to the case came to see me in the emergency room of the hospital, he and his partner practically begged me to make sure I reported to the police station to complete a written statement. Repeatedly he emphasized, how critical it was in prosecuting the case. Frequently, many people that were viciously attacked failed to follow through because they feared for their lives and the repercussion that could come from going forward. In other instances, it was just the desire of not wanting to revisit the trauma, because every time one visits the police concerning the matter it would force them to relive the details of the event.

I had dealt with all types of phobias, but I was not going to let anything cripple me from doing something that could potentially save others. I could not afford to let that man walk and be free to assault someone else! I was convinced that I was the voice for the weak and helpless! Although my motives seemed justifiable, I had to check my heart to see if I was fostering bitterness towards him in the process.

Keeping my heart pure by not harboring unforgiveness was difficult. On one occasion, when I met with the prosecutor to discuss the status of the case, I was informed about the plea bargain the defendant was offered. I remembered thinking, a plea bargain? How could the system cut a deal with this man? I wanted him to be tried; found guilty and sentenced for attempted murder, rape and robbery amongst other charges. I became very angry. This was not fair. Not after what he had done to me! I was flabbergasted! As the prosecutor tried to explain the law and how the judiciary system worked in prosecuting these types of criminal cases, I did not want to hear it. Then, in my rage, I heard an audible voice that silenced me.

"How much time would be enough for this young man? What would be a reasonable punishment for him? Is it death? Is it a life sentence? Twenty five years in prison or perhaps freedom?"

These questions defined the moment of truth for me. It jolted me. I had to ask myself where my heart was in the matter. I paused, pondered and searched my heart. Then I quietly answered,

"I don't know God. Only you know what would be a suitable punishment for him."

God sees the heart of every man. He sees the past, present and future. Only God knows the amount of time he needed to repent for what he had done and surrender his life to God. So I prayed;

"Father, take control of the judiciary process in this case. Allow the defendant to receive the sentencing equivocal to the amount of time needed for him to accept the wrong he had done, repent and turn his life over to You."

Instantly the compassion of God started tenderizing my heart towards this man. I began to have a desire to see him experience salvation. He was a lost soul. Just like I needed to forgive him, he needed to accept Jesus' forgiveness of his sins. Only the Holy Spirit can penetrate a hardened heart, melt it and turn it towards God Almighty. In other words, the Holy Spirit can raise a person's awareness to desire God's ways above their own. This would lead to one admitting that he or she is a sinner; repent by turning away from a sinful lifestyle and accepting a new life in Christ.

As God touched my heart I was able to forgive him. God gave me this incredible perspective to see the attacker with His eyes. I asked God to examine the depths of my heart and bring to my attention any bitterness I had towards this man for attacking me. I prayed;

"Search me oh God, cleanse me from all unrighteousness and make my heart pure before you. I repent of my unforgiveness and bitterness. Help me to release those who have hurt me including OW. Let your Spirit make this easy for me to accomplish experientially. Amen!"

And God answered my prayer!

Forgiving an individual or a group of people is easier, when we have godly people in our lives that hold us accountable to the standard of God. God had blessed me to be a part of a women's prayer group that met to pray for a few hours each month. During one of our prayer sessions, the Holy Spirit moved powerfully and everyone repented. It was amazing how the Holy Spirit exposed things that were hidden in our hearts. When it was my turn, I confessed about my weakened faith lately in believing that God was going to bring to pass all His promises for my life. Almost instantly, the host of the group turned to me and said;

"That's great but what about your attacker? Did you forgive him too?"

I paused, just long enough, to search my heart again, to see if I had any hidden unforgiveness towards him, but I found none. I praised God inwardly, and then I shared with the group how God's grace had supernaturally enabled me to forgive. I also thanked God for women who have had an honest desire to walk in the full purity of God, as well as helping others to do the same. I was truly grateful for this prayer group in my life.

As I journey with the Lord, I have come into the realization that when the Holy Spirit renews our spirit and creates a clean heart in us, we ought to bear good fruits. In other words, God usually tests the validity of the work that He does in the secret places. It was months after the attack and there was a court hearing in which the defendant was going to be making an appearance before the judge to hear the charges brought against him. It was also the first time I would see him since the day of the attack. I was not sure what my reaction would be. But all the people around me anticipated it would be difficult to look at the man that tried to kill me. Indeed, this was going to be a test to see if I had forgiven him.

OW was dressed in his prison attire, his ankles and wrists shackled in chains and cuffs, two policemen escorted him in the court room. As he stood before the judge, two additional police officers surrounded him. I was sitting about ten feet from where he was standing. When I saw him my heart filled with compassion for him. I saw emptiness and a mere shell of a man that had no sense of direction and purpose in society. He had no bridle of morality and so he did not care about right and wrong. He stood for nothing! So he was accessible ammunition the enemy could use and did use in my attack.

As I watched him from behind, I asked the Lord to have mercy and break the chains of wickedness off him. I also prayed for his salvation. By then, an officer came over to check if I was doing okay and my friend Shirley that accompanied me was looking at me intently to see if I was okay. I appreciated the concern, but I was fine. I did not feel awkward nor did I relive the symptoms of the attack. I praised God! Again, I saw the power of God demonstrated in such a real way in my heart and mind. Truly, I experienced the peace of God which surpasses all human understanding and I was able to forgive my attacker!

Chapter 9

°∞°∞°∞°∞°∞°∞°∞°∞°

Healing and Restoration

As I progressed along the road of recovery, I can truly say that God has miraculously healed me in multiple ways and continues to heal me of all residual effects from the trauma. I was very diligent in following up with my doctor's appointments, counseling sessions and the women's support group monthly meetings. I relied heavily on my friends and family's love, support and prayers to aide me through the process. As I experienced different issues during my recovery, it was important for me to be very honest about my feelings. I did not want to be like some super religious Christians that mask illness, hurt, pain, grief or disappointments because they do not want to appear as if they were not trusting God. This would be a false sense of Christianity. Being a Christian does not mean that one does not have troubles or experience difficult times. The Bible says;

> "For the righteous man may fall seven times..." -Proverb 24:16

> "The righteous cry out and the Lord hears. And delivers them out of all their troubles." -Psalm 34:17

I believe that I experienced a quick healing because I acknowledged and took all my burdens to the Lord and sought counsel when I needed it. A combination of Christian and secular counseling carried me through the initial trauma.

Although counseling is wonderful and I am in full support of it when necessary, I believe it also has the potential of keeping one in rehabilitation longer than necessary. My therapist was very surprised that I had moved through the phases of mental and emotional healing so quickly and was able to resume my routine. The therapist commented that it was quite unusual that someone recovers so quickly after going through such a traumatic experience. She could not figure it out, but I understood why. The natural man does not perceive the things of the Spirit of God, nor can he know them because they are spiritually discerned. Later in one of our sessions, the therapist said,

> "This is amazing. You exhibit such incredible strength. Your spirituality seems to work for you."

I said to myself;

> "Absolutely. My progress is only due to the intervening touch of God."

There is no man-made theory that can outdo God's creative power to heal and deliver. Although the therapist was not able to articulate what she sensed in me, she sensed that something was different in my healing. It was the Holy Spirit! Many times as I sat in counseling, the therapist would look at me in amazement. It was truly a miracle in every aspect of my story. Quickly, I progressed to a point, where I just wanted to move on with my life and not dwell on the attack, but I realized that my weekly counseling sessions were making it difficult for me to move on. Week after week, I was talking about the incident; almost forcing myself to find something that was off balanced in my psyche, which could be attributed to the attack. It became ridiculous after a while.

The sessions turned into probing questions about my childhood, and the relationship I had with my father and mother. Again this was another attempt to find some psychological component of my past that would justify and continue to rationalize why I responded or felt the way I did. It is not my intention to oversimplify or minimize the effectiveness of counseling. Counseling works, but I find that one of the problems with secular counseling is that it has the tendency to prolong pain, dig up the past, reexamine, justify the pain and keep you talking about the hurt when you need to put it to rest.

Additionally, psychotherapy sometimes promotes medication as a vital part of the recovery process. Again, this is good, but should not be abused. I had to take a stand on this issue. I was prescribed so much medication that was supposedly necessary to adjust my mental and physical equilibrium, that I could have developed an addiction. But by God's grace that did not happen. Medication is absolutely necessary in treating many mental imbalances; however, I wanted to trust God for supernatural healing. I had the secret answer that many health care practitioners wish they had. I had divine insight to know that once I talked about the incident and got it out of my system, the declarative power God gave through confession combined with faith in God; expedited the healing process. As I applied the Word of God to my wounds, healing manifested, because it is God that ultimately heals. Just rehearsing the events of the past did not bring about peace and healing. It is only God who is able to set free and deliver due to His mighty power. If one has poison trapped in an area under one's skin, just opening up the affected area is not enough to bring about healing. In fact, the area must be opened; the poison removed and the wound bound up, before the proper course of healing can manifest.

Emotional and psychological trauma affects the soul. Therefore, hurt that scars the soul needs more than drugs and talk therapy. It is the Holy Spirit that is able to surgically penetrate the ailing spot in the soul, uproot and soothe with the healing balm of Gilead. One of John Newton's Olney's hymns recognizes this and states;

> "There is a healing Balm in Gilead to save the sin sick soul."

This is powerful. That is why the Word of God has creative power. The Bible described it as living and powerful.

> "For the Word of God is living and powerful and sharper than any two edged sword; piercing even to the division of soul and spirits, and of joints and marrow; the soul and spirit and is a discerner of the thoughts and intents of heart." -Hebrews 4:12

This speaks of a power that is able to get to the root of the issue. There is no trial and error with God. The power of the Spirit of God is precise in its performance. This is demonstrated when people go through great tragedies and emerge whole. I have been to church services and have seen the power of God manifest in such a way that people with decades of emotional sufferings who have gone to doctors, had therapists, psychics, spiritual readers, turned to drugs, sex, alcohol, other worldly pleasures, utilized self-help books, felt barren, hurt and bound in their souls, were made whole in an instant after one encounter with God. This might seem far-fetched to some, but it is true! I have seen this with my own two eyes.

This phenomenon is almost like the biblical story of the woman that had a blood condition for many years. To be precise, the woman bled for 12 years. The Bible says she went to doctors, paid them all she had and still she was not cured. Then one day she heard about Jesus, this great healer in town and decided to see Him. Jesus was surrounded by throngs of people and was not very accessible but that did not deter this woman. She knew that the healing she had been trying to purchase all these years was in Christ. So by faith, she pressed her way through the crowds, believing that all she needed to do was to receive one touch from God. Indeed, she was right. One touch from God caused her to be healed instantly.

One touch from God is sufficient to bring about healing. There are times God will allow us to go through an extended healing process. However, God is still the ultimate healer. Sometimes the process is needed for us to appreciate the outcome. So whether healing is manifested quickly or over a long period of time, God promises to work things out on behalf of those that put their trust in Him.

> "All things work together for good to those who love the Lord and are called according to his purpose." -Romans 8:28

All things include your healing! I am often comforted by this promise, as I grapple with finding resolution in my inability to use my thumb completely, which affects my writing, overall hand strength and ability to perform seemingly simple fine motor skills. At times I even encounter things that I am unable to do due to the inhibited joint movement. This can be discouraging at times because it serves as a fresh reminder of a disability that I have to live with for the rest of my life. When I first realized that my tendon was not repaired, I remember saying;

> "Well, I am not going to worry about that, it will be repaired!"

But upon meeting with my surgeon and discussing the various possibilities and still none would guarantee the original joint movement, I was very disheartened. I had to resolve in my mind that God is still the Healer and He is in control. After agonizing for several weeks over my hand, I can say I have experienced God's grace and that changed how I looked at the healing of my hand. I now see my injury as the battle scar that I acquired in a fight against the evil one.

Sometimes a heroic soldier in war, experiences battle wounds that persist long after the battle is over. So I will not be hindered by the current limitations of my hand. I thank God for His grace that has caused me to currently see the miracle of God when I look at my hand! It is my battle scar that keeps me grounded, lest I forget. It is the scar that activates my faith when I doubt God. It is the visible sign that speaks volumes to my inner man and stirs me up to believe God again. A popular song says,

"If God does it once he will do it again."

In other words, our scars should serve as a reminder of a covenant between us and God. It marks a period of change or a turning point in our lives. It can be referred to as our limp.

This reminds me of when Jacob had an encounter with God and he refused to let God go until He blessed him. After an intense night of fighting, he had a limp and he never walked the same. One may choose to focus on the impairment of normal gait patterns or see it as the scar that defined the moment of truth. In that moment of history Jacob had an experience with the living God and he was destined not to walk the same. His limp was the reminder of how God blessed him. In fact, this marked his name change from Jacob to Israel.

What is your battle scar? Are you always hiding it? Are you allowing the enemy to suppress your opportunity to give God praise and encourage others about what God has done? Do not hide your scar. It marks the unveiling of a life that was redeemed from destruction. Scars reflect healing. It celebrates a defining moment in your life. It represents change. For many it marks a reshaping and molding of character, while for others it is the turning point of graduating from drinking milk to eating solid foods. Scars highlight greater spiritual depth. Don't be afraid of your scars. It marks healing. It is your proof of what God has done. Embrace them!

There is a clear distinction between healing and restoration although related. Healing refers to being made whole again, as in the case of repairing that which is broken, while restoration refers to a replenishing of that which was loss due to an injury. Besides the money that was taken from me during the attack, which would be considered a loss; there was a personal loss that I experienced, which was intangible. I felt defeated. A loss of self confidence and assurance of safety were only a few of the struggles I had to overcome. There was an incomprehensible brokenness in my soul that needed to be restored! I lost emotional and psychological ground. I needed to be replenished.

The need for restoration was so great. For me it was more than just physical remedy. Restoration was essential for me to resume a healthy and productive lifestyle. This was not a natural fix. It required divine intervention. There were days when the essence of who I was, felt very unstable and insecure. I could not recognize me. At least, I did not feel like me. This is one of the worst feelings a person could go through. Imagine waking up to someone other than the real you; and you know it, but you are unable to do anything about it. Finding myself in this predicament, reminded me of something that my High School principal would say at the beginning of the school's assembly on Monday mornings. When I was in High School, the statement had no meaning. However, as I matured, it came to mean so much and almost revolutionized my perspective on life, health and wellness. She said;

> "I thank God for waking me up this morning in my right mind and I know it and can appreciate it"

What a simple, yet profound statement. I have had days I was so distressed to in my soul. I did not know if I were coming or going. In moments like these, the Restorer of our lives saw the missing parts and replaced them.

Have you ever been downcast and did not know why? If you are like me, the answer is yes! And so God is the one who searches and replenishes us. Day by day, after the incident, I sought to rediscover me. It was a deliberate act on my part to resume my routine. Besides not remembering what I did and when I did what, I had no drive or desire to get back to my routine. However, with the help of the Holy Spirit, He enabled me to purpose in my heart to do a little at a time in reclaiming my life. So, like an individual learning to walk again, I had to learn to live again. I did the best I could, but still that was not enough.

I had to cultivate the presence of God in my life, which was critical in my restoration. I had to create more opportunities where I was lost in worship. There were times I would lay on the floor of my living room and sing worship songs unto the Lord until I received what I needed from Him. There were other times, I had no strength, I just had to lay by my CD player and play worship songs that ushered in the presence of God for as long as it took to feel the touch of God. During those times, I come to love this simple song by Matt Redman;

> "How lovely is your dwelling place, your love is restoring my soul. I am yours and you are mine, so from this heart a song will rise, I love you, I love you, I love you."

For me power came from knowing that the love of God definitively restores us. His love for me restored me. At times, I would become teary-eyed as I thought about how much God loves me. He continues to fill me up when I ask. Sometimes,

I do not ask because I do not know what I need. Nevertheless, He comes and fills me with fresh courage; stirs my ability to dream; grants new insight and strength to run again. He even gives the ability to feel good within. Many times people ask as an expression of greeting how one is doing. Usually people nonchalantly respond out of custom;

"Fine. Thank you."

But are you really fine? And if you are fine, do you praise God that you are fine? I had a friend who accused me of projecting a religious spirit, when I am asked how I was doing; I chose to say;

"I am fine. Praise God!"

In fact, my only reason for responding this way is because, I do not ever want to forget that God is the one that enables me to feel good in my soul or cause me to be at peace. I have had great sorrows and disappointments in my life. As a result, I have experienced tremendous agony and sadness. So, I praise God when I feel good. Weeks after the attack, I was at church, when an individual had asked me how I was doing and I said;

"Good. Praise God!"

Caught up in her own thoughts the person went on about her business, as if I had said nothing. I remember going after the individual, with a fuse of excitement and said;

> "You don't understand. I have searched myself, and I feel good. So, I praise God! I said this because there were many days I had not felt this good. In fact, that day was the first day I felt good, in a long time."

The person nodded, showing appreciation for the time I took to share my testimony. So the next time you communicate how good you are doing, take time to acknowledge God whether inwardly or outwardly; give God the praise!

Restoration was multi-faceted for me, as I moved on with my life. I thank the Lord that His mercies are new every morning, and so He continued to supply my every need. These needs were not just material things but also included emotional stability, psychological wellness, inner peace, strength, assurance and safety. So as I remained mindful of the numerous needs I had, I also had to depend on God and take Him at His

Word. That is why the songwriter of one of the old hymns of the church, Louisa M. R. Stead wrote;

"It's so sweet to trust in Jesus,
Oh to take Him at His Word,
Jesus, Jesus, precious Jesus,
Oh for grace to trust you more."

In Psalm 103:2, the Psalmist reminds me;

"Bless the Lord, oh my soul and forget not all His benefits."

This includes restoration for everything the enemy had stolen. God will give back a thousand-fold. It is my inheritance and that is not because I said it and I desire it, but because God said it! And I believe Him! Is there a loss you have experienced? In God's Word, He promises;

"So I will restore the years that the swarming, crawling, consuming and chewing locusts have eaten." -Joel 2:25

As He does this, the latter rain is going to be greater than the former rain. God establishes his covenant forever, so we can be glad and rejoice because the Lord has done marvelous things. And he will cause the rain to come for you. What do you want God to restore? Let faith arise in your heart to believe. Is it a job, a business, career, ministry, finances, spouse, provision for your household, children, salvation for a loved one, a broken marriage or relationship?

> "You shall know that I am in your midst"
> -Joel 2:27

> "Your threshing floor will be full of wheat and your vats will overflow with new oil."
> -Joel 2:24

> "You will eat plenty and be satisfied, and praise the name of the Lord!" -Joel 2: 26

In the book of Joel 2:27, it also reads;

> "I am the Lord your God. And there is no other. My people shall never be put to shame!"

So, wait on God and your time of replenishing will come. The prophet Isaiah states;

> "Those that wait upon the Lord shall be renewed in strength. They shall mount up

with wings like eagles, they shall run and not be weary, they shall walk and not faint."
- Isaiah 40:31

"Wait I say, on the Lord." -Psalm 27:14

Chapter 10

°∞°∞°∞°∞°∞°∞°∞°∞°

A Deeper Level of Submission

Submission refers to an intentional and deliberate yielding of one's self to a person, item or cause. Submitting to God requires brokenness and yielding in one's heart, which enables a person to subject self to the Will of God. Understanding that a person has a body, soul and spirit, when one accepts Christ as the head of one's life, a transformation takes place in the heart and that person is considered born again. Subsequently, the body is now governed by the Spirit of God.

Being led by the Spirit encompasses a sincere desire to see God's Kingdom come and His Will be done in our lives. In fact, it is a new level of awakening and consciousness that allows one to be used in the unfolding of God's plan. As in my own experience, dealing with the attack, picking up the pieces and pressing to move on with life, a new strength is emerging. I am a new woman. Out of my shattered self-confidence, an unshakable confidence in God has arisen in me! It has caused me to take my self-imposed limits off God. Abraham asked;

"Is there anything too hard for the Lord?"

Nothing is too hard for the Lord. Throughout this process, I realized that a lack of confidence in God breathes fear, which inhibits one's focus and overall productivity. Boldness is priceless in the life of a Christian. I am reminded of a dear friend, who said on multiple occasions,

"I fear no man!"

He states this declaratively, definitively, emphatically and authoritatively. It was refreshing to see his confidence and assurance in God. As I sat across the table from him, with extreme admiration, I nodded in full agreement, because he recognized as well as I did that if we reverence God, there is a boldness we obtain which surpasses any special gifts or training a person might have received. The scriptures states, we are to fear only the One that is able to destroy both body and soul. Only God can destroy the body and soul! There is a quickening that the Holy Spirit does, that drives out all fear. That is why Timothy says;

> "God has not given us a spirit of fear, but of power and love and a sound mind."
> -2 Timothy 1:7

Submission to God causes us to walk in power that is beyond human intelligence. When we walk in the power of God, we are able to battle giants like Goliath, in our lives, because we are not scared. Imagine if David had been afraid of Goliath. Would he have been able to slay the giant? Absolutely not! However, we cannot overlook David's submission to God. It positioned him so that God Almighty could demonstrate His power through him. Interestingly, David's submission catapulted him into the blessings that God had prepared for his life.

I wish submission was easy, but truthfully, submission calls for dying to self. John 12: 24 states;

"Unless a grain of wheat goes into the earth and dies, it remains alone, but if it dies, it produces much grain."

True submission denies self to do the Will of the Father. Submission requires people with hearts that are receptive and in tune with God's heart. A person that has a submitted heart has ears that hear the Will of God. Denying self is difficult because the natural tendency of man is selfish. It pleases us to gratify self and so most times we refuse to deny ourselves. Submission takes us out of our comfort zone. It can be very uncomfortable. It is comparable to stripping the layers of an onion. Dying to self requires a peeling away of selfish ambitions. Self prevents many from living lives that are submitted to the fullness of God's plan. God gave us free will. As a result, He does not force us into submission, or else that would be control, which is a spirit that is grounded in witchcraft practices. Instead, His love for us draws us to desire His way for our lives. Sometimes, when we choose contrarily to His plan for our lives, His love constrains us in

His will. Eventually His Spirit convicts us to desire His will.

Now more than ever in my life, I am experiencing the constraints of God that makes me want to submit. For years I would pray;

"Constrain me in your will God at all costs."

Therefore, submitting to the Lord was going to come one way or another. The attack had caused my heart to become more tenderized towards God. There was a breaking of my will that caused me to say,

"Your will be done Lord and not mine."

You know as well as I do, how we can strive in our own strength, especially if we are highly motivated. This type of brokenness has caused a refreshing humility in my attitude and spirit, where I just want to do God's will. I have an intense desire to press into the things of God. There is fresh zeal to be holy and set apart for God's service. I want to be purposeful and diligent about God's business, while remaining in position for Him to use me. Jesus exemplifies this when he was as young as twelve years old when he went to Jerusalem with his parents. Driven by purpose, Christ went into the temple and remained there. His parents could not find Him. So voicing their parental concern, they enquired of Jesus;

"Where were you?"

So, like any purpose driven person, Jesus answered;

"Why do you seek Me? Did you not know that I must be about my Father's business?" -Luke 2:49

So, if Jesus, who is God himself, had this urgency, who are we not to follow his example? Time is running out. We must be busy about the things of the Father!

The attack had caused my roots to be deeper in God. There was an anchoring in my soul where I could now believe God for the impossible. My faith has been strengthened. The attack had evoked faith in me to believe God for everything!

"If you have faith and do not doubt....if you say to this mountain, be removed and be cast into the sea, it will be done." -Matthew 21:21

We need to remind ourselves;

"Without faith, it is impossible to please God..."
-Hebrews 11:6

Sometimes it seemed easier said than done when we encountered the pressures of life. Life can be riddled with situations that can rattle our faith to the point of disbelief. In those moments when it is difficult to trust God, we need to be honest with God. Like the man that asked Jesus if He could do anything to heal his son. And Jesus answered;

"If you can believe all things are possible to him that believes." -Mark 9:23

This pointed directly to the father's faith level. And he knew it and immediately repented and said;

"Lord, please help my unbelief." -Mark 9:24

Then his son was healed! So when the storms of life arise and you cannot see how you will survive shipwreck, ask the Lord for faith to believe Him. If there are areas of your life, where you cannot muster the faith to believe God for breakthrough, you must pray;

"Heavenly Father, with you all things are possible, so remove my unbelief and grant me faith to believe by the power of Jesus' Name. Amen!"

The incident deepened my conviction for Christ. Queen Esther was convinced beyond measure in her heart, that she must do all she could to save her people even if it meant death. She said;

"If I perish, I perish." -Esther 4:16

Esther realized that the cause was too great to be taken lightly. Like an insatiable hunger, I have a new desperation for God. It has led me to Godly repentance which brought me into a deeper level of intercession, worship and obedience. I have a renewed passion for Christ. Now, I am fully determined to get everything God has in store for me. There is a driving power that forces me not to give up. It is known as sustaining power. God has done too much for me to quit now. So, if you had quit your original assignment, repent and get back on track. There are great things in store!

God is result oriented and so He wants returns on His investment in you. You have to stay the course in order to deliver and experience the joy of birth. Imagine a mother conceiving a baby and carrying the baby for nine months and never giving birth. It would be a travesty! Eventually the healthy full term baby would die. So do not abort the plans of God for your life!

Chapter 11

°∞°∞°∞°∞°∞°∞°∞°∞°

The Resolution

God wants us to literally take him at His Word. His Word breathes life. It accomplishes God's intentions. That is why the scripture says,

"So shall my Word that goes forth from My mouth; It shall not return to Me void, but it shall accomplish what I please." -Isaiah 55:11

This is an infallible promise! God's Word in our lives will do all that He has purposed it to do. In fact, we can only receive the promises (blessings) of the Lord if we believe His Word. Therefore, faith is the fuel that activates the Word of God into manifested blessings. Although it is different experientially for each person, God gives us all a certain measure of faith. Use your faith to overcome. Build your faith by listening to the testimonies of others. Reflect on past victories in your life and encourage yourself in the scriptures.

I praise God for allowing me to see the mighty hand of God in a powerful way, even as the Israelites experienced the parting of the Red Sea that brought them to safety as the sea swallowed up their enemies. God promises His own, that no evil shall come to them. Only with their eyes shall they behold the rewards of the wicked. The enemy's plots will not destroy God's children. There is nothing more awesome than to see God move on our behalf. It puts the scriptures in action. This is the demonstrative power of God!

Despite the multi-faceted trials that came from the attack (a series of trials within a trial), I glorify God for proving His Word to me in a personal way. I am resolved that God is 'The Power' of all powers. He is the same God that moved on Israel's behalf to bring down great kings and hand over nations to them for His

Name sake, is the same God that works on our behalf. I have seen the impossible moved by the hand of God.

I understand experientially that God is a present help in time of trouble. He acts swiftly and is always on time. I have come to understand the safety we have in God when we commit our lives to Him. This is a lifetime guaranteed warranty that was bought with the blood of Christ! I believe God for anything and everything now. My faith in God has enhanced my life as an intercessor. I have a righteous indignant disposition that arises in prayer, which makes me pray fervently against the powers of darkness. This new fervency has caused me to step into another dimension of prayer. I understand the reality of the forces of good and evil operating in our society. Evil spirits are in constant opposition against the Will of God, seeking to frustrate or ultimately destroy God's established purposes. Such principalities have taken over regions of our cities. There is an unbelievable hierarchy of evil that exists in the spiritual realm. That is why the Bible reminds us that we wrestle not against flesh and blood but against spiritual wickedness in high places. Just imagine that evil is more predisposed and pervasive in certain areas because of the territorial principality that exists over certain regions. Understanding this we need to pray more fervently. I am more determined to upset the gates of hell through prayer. Prayer is our weapon of warfare which is mighty in pulling down strongholds. Chuck Pierce said;

> "The quality of our Christian life should be determined by how much fear we cause in satan's camp."

I want to be the type of Christian that makes hell tremble. Still, it comes back to prayer. Prayer is the force that moves God to release His power to intercept evil. In fact, answering the call to intercessory prayer could make the difference between life and death.

Dr. Judy who is a dear friend and prayer warrior was a part of a monthly women's prayer group that I frequently attended. However, the Wednesday night before the Friday of the attack, I attended midweek church service at Christ Church. After a full day at work, I just wanted to leave church quickly, without any fellowshipping as soon as the service ended. Trying to sneak through the door, I bumped into Dr. Judy. Excited, we stopped to greet each other.

Just as Dr. Judy leaned forward to embrace me, the presence of God fell and she began praying fervently in her heavenly language. Somewhat aware of our surrounding, we tried to bring our meeting to an end, but the Spirit of the Lord formed such a thick cloud that consumed us and we could not get out of His presence quickly. Being the fire ball she is for God, she laid hands on me and prayed for God's divine protection over my life. I felt the wind of heaven in that encounter. It almost seemed strange, but I knew it was God so I did not resist. I could not explain this, but I knew that this type of prayer was different. This was going to change something in my life. The intense prayer lasted for about fifteen minutes by the door. Finally, we hugged and parted.

Two days later, that Friday, I was attacked and miraculously survived. One week later, I remembered that it was the Wednesday night before the attack that Dr. Judy had specifically prayed for God's protection for me. I was beside myself. Immediately, I had an urgency to get in touch with her and speak to her about the attack. After leaving messages at all her contact numbers, she finally called me. Over the phone I informed her about the details of the incident. She listened quietly and intently. When I was finished, she praised God with me and thanked him for sparing my life. We hung up. Moments later she called me back and said, she was so overwhelmed with emotions from my story and was in awe of God's power. She needed a moment to process what happened. This was when she shared the other part of the puzzle to my story. Dr. Judy revealed the following;

"I have been having nightmares since July of 2007. And the nightmare involved the same recurring dream. I could not understand it, so I tried to ignore it, but as time went on, the dream became more graphic. It was a dream of a young woman being attacked by a man with a knife. I thought it probably had to do with unresolved fear from my past. Still the dream did not seem relevant to my life. Anyway, the dream persisted for weeks and would often wake me up in cold sweat, accompanied by a fear that paralyzed me. I started to sense that this dream was different. I did not have the answers but I felt that the dream had great significance. So I started seeking God about what it meant. I prayed for a while but received no

insight. I thought it was strange and decided not to worry about it. So I went on with life.

Then there was a spiraling of events that started happening in my life. I had trouble on every side. I felt like I was in the wind of misfortune. I cried out to God and asked Him, if He had forgotten me. It was truly a Job experience. I had no refuge but Jesus. I was desperate for God to move on my behalf. I started praying more fervently and fasting. The more I fasted and prayed for the situations in my life, interestingly, the more vivid the dream of the man attacking the woman became. Then I understood that God wanted me to pray against this attack. So I started interceding strategically as time progressed.

One day, I was going home from work late. It could have been about 1:30 A. M. I took the bus from the city and had to walk a few blocks to my house after I got off the bus. So in the wee hours of the morning, as I was walking home, I had a vision of the same reoccurring nightmare. It was so clear. It was as if it was happening right before my eyes that moment. I saw a young woman, being pinned to the ground by a man dressed in black with a knife in his hand, attempting to slit her throat and the woman was frantically screaming for help.

Immediately, I felt like I was supernaturally lifted up in the Spirit, and I started calling on the Name of the Lord. I rebuked the evil spirit, saying she shall live and not die in the Name of Jesus! I kept on calling out, she shall live! She shall live! With hate and intent to kill her, he persisted, but as I prayed I could see him losing his strength, so I kept praying in the power of God. When the evil one was bound, the woman's deliverance came. Suddenly, the man dropped his knife and ran. It was evident that God showed up on her behalf and saved her life.

Stepping out of the intense spiritual battle I walked home, amazed at the awesomeness of God, but still perplexed as to who this young woman was. Then when you called me and described the attack, I realized that you were the young woman, God had me interceding for."

Awestruck, by the power of God, we broke out in a round of praise and thanksgiving. Moments later, while we were still on the phone, Dr. Judy received an incoming call. The phone call resolved all the delays and trials that she was experiencing for weeks, which led her to fervent prayer and fasting. God instantaneously fixed Dr. Judy's problems. But it was important that He created enough ruffling in her life to get her to a point to intercede, which in turn, saved my life.

To pray is life and to neglect prayer is death. Sometimes the struggles in our lives are not ours, but they are for people God wants to use us to deliver. We must be wise to the tricks of the enemy. He tries to consume us with grief about our problems, to the point of immobilization, where we cannot pray for others. Also, know that while we are praying for others, God has placed us on someone else's heart to be prayed for. So we are never lacking in prayer! I have learned that when God places someone on our hearts to pray for, we must pray! We never know what plot of the enemy we are unfolding or weakening. Prayer is serious and we must be serious about taking up our places on the wall! So, I am resolved to pray as God leads me to pray!

As life went on, I moved from the place where I was attacked. Now I have a greater appreciation for life and see the importance of living it to the fullest. I have decided to be more deliberate in my approach towards enjoying life. So often, I find myself putting off pleasure with the underlying feeling that I am young and I have time to enjoy life later, but I realize that tomorrow is not promised. So never put off the things that can be done today for tomorrow! Likewise, enjoy your family, friends, loved ones, health, strength and the prosperity that God has blessed you with. Make the best of every moment. We must learn to live in the present, not recklessly, but with wisdom and proper balance. We should build vacation time in our lives and take breaks from work periodically. There is some truth in the adage that says;

"All work and no play make Jack dull."

I have decided not to be burdened by trivial matters. I refuse to spend my time and energy on anything that detracts from the uplifting of my spirit.

Now I look for more ways to love, laugh, fulfill my purpose and enjoy God's creation. Life is too short. We owe it to God and to ourselves to have fun. Be happy!

"A merry heart is good, like medicine."
-Proverb 17:22

Take a moment to examine your life and find the situations that are preventing you from enjoying life the way God intended. Pray about it and then take action as God brings it to your attention. Draining the poison of sadness and unfulfillment from one's life brings longevity. God's intent for our lives is clear. Jesus came so that we may live an abundant life! Do not be afraid! Enjoy living!

Chapter 12

°∞°∞°∞°∞°∞°∞°∞°∞°

New Beginnings

Two years had almost passed since the attack had occurred. It was a bright and sunny morning. It was a perfect spring day, Friday, May 8, 2009. I had been waiting for this day to come, so I could move on with my life. I did not stop living but there was an inner resolution I needed to put the matter at rest. It was the day of sentencing for my attacker. The day of vindication had finally arrived. I pondered,

"Wow the day is finally here. I waited a long time for this."

I was in a solemn and pensive mood, so I decided to spend some extended time in prayer. As I thought about the journey leading up to this day, tears welled up in my eyes. God had taken me from a long way. I was a woman that was broken, hard pressed on every side and crushed in spirit, yet I was being built up again. I have endured and overcome much pain and suffering with this ordeal, but God faithfully carried me out of the valley. My heart was filled with deep gratitude to Almighty God for how He preserved my life from death and shame. I tried to hold back the tears because I did not want to become too flustered before I appeared in court that day. As I knelt in prayer, I prayed for strength and courage to face the events that would come later that morning.

Feeling refreshed, energized and assured, I got off my knees and got dressed. I brushed my hair into a neat bun. I wore an elegant white long sleeve, fitted silk shirt, dark brown satin pant, matching stilettos and a belt which was accented with a white pearl necklace and earrings. As I applied gold tone lip gloss and checked myself one final time in the mirror, I straightened my shoulders, stood tall and smiled confidently. Picked up my purse and walked to my car.

I started pondering about what I would say when I addressed the court. I silently prayed;

"Dear God, Give me the words to speak, so I may honor your Name. Amen."

In evenly paced strides, I walked into the court building and stood in front of the courtroom, double-checked the courtroom number on the door and then entered. It was a small and typical courtroom. Approximately fifteen people were already seated in addition to the judge, lawyers and other court administrative staff. I walked in, quickly scanned the room and decided on an unobtrusive seat towards the back of the court room. At about the same time, I saw the prosecutor, who came over to speak to me. Even though I had wished the circumstances under which we met her were different, I must admit she was a delightful young woman. I have much respect and appreciation for what she had done for me during this trial. She was always very professional in her demeanor, yet very warm and compassionate. We both greeted each other with firm handshakes and warm smiles. After a moment of friendly exchange, she reminded me of what to expect and assured me that today's proceedings would not take long because there were only a few other cases ahead of me. Concluding our conversation, she went to the front of the court room, while I sat in the back and waited for my case to be called.

As I waited and watched the proceedings from the other cases going forth, there was a tangible presence of the Holy Spirit in the court room. It was a peace that transcends all understanding. My mind wondered about different things, in between judgments and sentencing. But in the midst of my thoughts, I could not help noticing the judge, an exceptionally beautiful Black woman, tall, slender and graceful looking. She had very high cheek bones and well proportioned facial features, tapered with soft and tasteful touches of makeup. She looked like a queen. I remember saying to myself;

> "This woman has an appearance that is divinely royal."

Although her beauty was captivating, I was particularly impressed with how firm she was, yet just and compassionate. She spoke with authority and wisdom. I marveled at the wisdom that was bestowed upon her and concluded in my mind that she had to be saved, because her counsel was not ordinary. That type comes from above. As the court agenda moved along, I realized that most of the people that were prosecuted were minority men, ranging from ages 18 to 50 years old, one Black man, after the next. The epidemic of incarceration is more pervasive among Black men, than many realize. I began to think about the recent statistics I heard. It was expected that at least 80% of Black men will not be productive in society. In other words, four out of every five Black men will not be successful. This daunting expectation broke my heart. I thought about my attacker. He was only 28 years-old when he attacked me, and prior to that, he had a long rap sheet, that stretched back to his teenage years. As I considered the social plight that erodes the fabric of society, it is the children that are caught in this vicious cycle. Almost all the men that came before the judge had children. Even my attacker had a fifteen year old son.

My thoughts were interrupted by the prosecutor coming over to whisper,

"The defendant will be coming in the courtroom in five minutes."

I braced myself, psychologically. Moments later, the defendant was brought in. He stood before the judge, in handcuffs and leg restraints. Upon his entrance into the courtroom, a middle-aged man and woman moved to the first row on the right hand side of the court room. I later learned that they were relatives of the defendant. The woman was his mother and the man was his uncle. I sat quietly in my seat praying that God would give me the grace to remain calm.

The judge went over the details of the sentencing for the attacker, which turned out to be eight years, serving a mandatory 85% of the sentenced time before eligibility for parole. After the logistics were completed, the judge spoke sternly to the defendant about letting this be the last time he is involved with anything that is criminal. She advised him to take advantage of various programs that would equip him with the skills he would need to live a different lifestyle when he is released from jail. The judge cautioned him that if he is truly serious about changing his life, the decisions he makes now will change his future. The defendant listened attentively and answered, nodding his head in full agreement.

"Yes Ma'am,"

After the judge finished speaking the defendant's mother asked to address the court. The judge beckoned her to the bench. Overcome with emotions, she whispered to the judge through her tears;

"Thank you."

She paused, sighed heavily and took a deep breath to gain composure, and then she started speaking. She explained that she had done her best as a single parent raising the defendant who chose to live a life of crime starting from a very young age. She went on to mention that she hopes this time he changes and reorders his life so that he can be a better father to his teenage son. She ended her address by letting the defendant know that she was not proud of what he had done but she will never stop loving him. When she was finished speaking, she sobbed bitterly in her hands as she made her way back to her seat.

The judge then called for me to come to the front to give my Victim Impact Statement. As I made my way to the front, a flood of emotions came over me. My day in court had come, where I would look the defendant in the eye and tell him exactly what he had done to me. I stood before the judge and stated my name and slowly proceeded to say;

"I have come a long way since the attack two years ago. Besides permanent injury to my hand, which limits my hand function, the trauma from the violent attack had caused great emotional pain which I am actively working through. I give praise to Almighty God for His grace over my life that kept me that day and continues to heal me."

Then I turned to the defendant and said;

"If I could say anything of substance to you, it is to remind you that today marks the start of a new day for you. I forgive you. Now there are two roads before you, one leads to good and the other leads to evil. Choose well. Choose good! God is giving you a second chance."

By then, I could not hold back the tears. Tears streamed down my face. I could not speak. I was asked if I wanted to stop but I shook my head and said;

"No, I will be okay."

The court allowed me some time to bare my soul into a facial tissue before I continued speaking.

> *"Ladies and gentlemen, prison is supposed to rehabilitate a prisoners' mind, but more often than not, prisoners are worst coming out than going in, but I pray that you will be the exception. Choose good! My heart goes out to your fifteen year old son. He is the same age as the boys I teach. Like so many other boys, he will not benefit from not having his father in his life during this critical period. In fact, it is in this age group many boys begin to drop out of school and without the necessary academic skills, survival is almost impossible due to limited opportunities. Frustration will set in and in a desperate attempt to survive, many turn to crime. Being here today, you have reminded me of the integral role I play in molding, shaping and inspiring the minds of boys to embrace academic success and increase their life options, so they will never be left to the mercies of a broken legal system. As an educator, I am more determined to fight a little harder to save the minority boys I teach in the Inner City. Thank you."*

The potency of every word spoken pierced the atmosphere, as the message behind the words lingered. There was a hush over the court room. If a pin dropped it would have been heard. When I finished speaking, not a dry eye was left in the room, as I walked to my seat. The defendant then asked to speak. The judge granted permission. He turned and looked at me and said;

"I apologize Miss Brown for hurting you."

Then he turned to his mother and said;

"Ma, thank you for all you have done for me. It is not your fault why I am here. It is on me. You have done your best."

To the man, he briefly acknowledged and said,

"Thank you."

The judge concluded the session. The defendant was taken away and the court recessed for lunch.

I waited to thank the prosecutor for her hard work and diligence is bringing about vindication. I was so grateful. I repeatedly thanked her. She smiled graciously and responded,

"It is my job."

We shook hands, offered well wishes and parted. I quickly gathered my bag and walked out of the courtroom. Just outside the door, I was met by the relatives of the defendant. His mother came to me, extended her hand and introduced herself as the defendant's Mom and said;

"I just want to let you know that I am truly sorry for what my son did to you and I wish you all the best as you move on with your life. Thank you for all the words you spoke today."

Feeling awkward, I reluctantly shook her hand, then looked in her face and saw the pain of a mother's broken heart, glazed with deep sorrow in her eyes. In a small cracked voice, I said;

"Thank you. I wish you all the best too."

I shrugged my shoulders, turned and walked away with impressions of their sad faces on my heart. Moved with compassion, I prayed silently;

"God have mercy on this family."

I exhaled. Leaving my past behind, I walked out of the municipal building; ready to embrace new beginnings.

About The Author

°∞°∞°∞°∞°∞°∞°∞°∞°

Nadeen Patricia Brown was born in Jamaica, West Indies and currently resides in New Jersey. She is a licensed school administrator, certified Biology and General Science teacher, intercessor, worship leader, song writer as well as the founder of NPB Greetings which delivers inspirational greeting cards and a Summer Science Program.

Nadeen has a passion for life and uses her gifts to bless many people in song, intercession, speaking engagements, personalized plaques and greeting cards.

Contact Information

°∞°∞°∞°∞°∞°∞°∞°∞°

Website: www.divineworks.org

Email:nadeenbrown@divineworks.org

Mailing Address: P. O. Box 2008,
East Orange, NJ 07019